AMAZING STORIES

JOHN LENNON

AMAZING STORIES

JOHN LENNON

Music, Myth and Madness

BIOGRAPHY

by Nate Hendley

This book is dedicated to Alyson Fischer,
whose hand I want to hold.

PUBLISHED BY ALTITUDE PUBLISHING CANADA LTD.
1500 Railway Avenue, Canmore, Alberta T1W 1P6
www.altitudepublishing.com
1-800-957-6888

First published 2005

Publisher	Stephen Hutchings
Associate Publisher	Kara Turner
Series Editor	Jill Foran
Editor	Geoff McKenzie
Digital Photo Colouring	Bryan Pezzi

We acknowledge the financial support of the Government of Canada through the Book Publishing Industry Development Program (BPIDP) for our publishing activities.

Altitude GreenTree Program
Altitude Publishing will plant twice as many trees as were used in the manufacturing of this product.

National Library of Canada Cataloguing in Publication Data

Hendley, Nate
John Lennon / Nate Hendley.

(Amazing stories)
ISBN 1-55265-902-X

1. Lennon, John, 1940-1980. 2. Rock musicians--England--Biography.
I. Title. II. Series: Amazing stories (Canmore, Alta.)

ML420.L567H45 2005 782.42166'092 C2005-901005-3

Printed and bound in Canada by Friesens
2 4 6 8 9 7 5 3 1

Contents

Prologue 9
Chapter 1 Come Together 10
Chapter 2 Love Me Do 24
Chapter 3 Ticket to Ride. 41
Chapter 4 Here, There and Everywhere 52
Chapter 5 Summer of Love 62
Chapter 6 Across the Universe 77
Chapter 7 The Ballad of John and Yoko 89
Chapter 8 The Plastic Ono Band 101
Chapter 9 New York, New York 112
Chapter 10 Starting Over 126
Epilogue 137
Further Reading 140

Prologue

John Lennon paced backstage, an anxious figure dressed in white with long hair and a beard. He idly strummed an electric guitar that was strapped over his shoulder. In a few minutes, he would play his first full-fledged solo concert without the Beatles.

He surveyed his backup band, hastily assembled in London only hours earlier. His superstar guitarist, Eric Clapton, was laid out on the ground behind the Toronto stage, having just resuscitated from a drug-induced stupor. Lennon didn't feel much better himself. Perhaps if the band had had time for a proper rehearsal...

His new wife, Yoko Ono, hung close to his side. The Japanese avant-garde artist had become John's constant companion. They had made music and created art together. Now, he was relying on her to firm up his shaky nerves.

Lennon adjusted his gold-rimmed glasses and ran a pick over his guitar strings. So much had changed in the music world since the Beatles had stopped touring in 1966. Would audiences still like his music? Could the band manage a set?

In the distance, Lennon could hear the expectant screams of the crowd. A stagehand stepped forward and motioned to Lennon. It was time.

Flashing his wife a weak smile, he roused his ragged band – Clapton too – and led them, hearts pounding, into the uproar.

Chapter 1
Come Together

Searchlights crisscrossed the night sky above Liverpool, probing the darkness for Nazi bombers. Screeching air raid sirens filled the air as residents rushed into bomb shelters. Nervous soldiers scanned the sky in front of their anti-aircraft guns, awaiting the signal to open fire on enemy planes.

It was 9 October 1940 and the height of the Blitz – the German effort to raze Britain's cities from the air. As a major port that was host to ships from around the world, Liverpool was a particularly tempting target. The Nazis were doing their best to raze the city and pulverise its docks.

Meanwhile, in Liverpool Maternity Hospital, Julia Lennon was fighting a different kind of battle. Julia, who was 27 years old, had been in labour for an entire day. Her husband, Freddie

Lennon, was away at sea and not at her side.

After what seemed like an endless struggle, her son was born. Julia named him John and pondered what life was going to be like now that she was a mother and her country – and her husband – were at war.

* * *

Julia Lennon had long auburn hair and an attractive face. She was flirty, spirited and – in the opinion of her strait-laced sister, Mimi Smith – terribly immature.

Julia's husband Freddie was also high-spirited and happy-go-lucky. Freddie was a ham who loved to crack jokes and show off. The pair met as teenagers. They married in December 1938.

Liverpool was a tough town, but with the war effort gearing up, there were jobs to be had at the factories and docks that dominated this working class city. Freddie worked as a ship's steward. Following the outbreak of World War II, he became a merchant seaman. It was a dangerous occupation; British ships were under constant threat from prowling German U-boats.

In late 1940, with a new baby and her husband away, Julia had to fend for herself. At first she lived with her parents, then moved to a cottage she rented from Mimi's husband.

Julia took to the single life with enthusiasm – but she proved to be less of a natural at parenting. Away from her own parents and her husband, the young mother spent her time in local pubs, dancing and flirting with sailors and soldiers. John spent many nights alone.

By 1944, Julia had taken up with a handsome Welsh soldier named Taffy Williams, and his friend John Dykins. Julia, Taffy and John liked to drink and party. Before long, Julia became pregnant with Taffy's child.

In June 1945, a few weeks after the war ended, Julia had her second baby. She gave the child up to a Liverpool Salvation Army orphanage with a distinctive name: Strawberry Field.

With the infant out of the way, Julia turned her sites on a new target: John Dykins. Little John Lennon began experimenting with temper tantrums.

In March 1946, Freddie Lennon finally returned home. He was aware of Julia's fling with Taffy Williams and her subsequent pregnancy, but Julia's affair with John Dykins came as a rude surprise. With young John looking on in bewilderment, Dykins and Freddie got into a fight. Dykins won. Bruised and humiliated, Freddie went back to sea.

Later that spring, Freddie returned to Liverpool again. Upon learning that his son was living temporarily with his Aunt Mimi, Freddie paid the boy a visit. Freddie wanted to take John to Blackpool. Reluctantly, Mimi agreed. John enjoyed several idyllic weeks with Freddie, going on amusement park rides, walking along the beach and being close to the father he barely knew.

Like countless other post-war Britons, Freddie wanted

to emigrate and start over in a brand-new country. He made plans to move to New Zealand – and take John with him. But before he could make good on his plans, Julia showed up in Blackpool. As irresponsible as she was, Julia wasn't about to see her son packed off to New Zealand. And in case Freddie had any lingering doubts, Julia made one thing clear: their marriage was over and Freddie wasn't welcome in her home.

But what to do with John? As both parents wanted custody they hit upon what seemed to them like a sensible solution: set the five-year-old John in the centre of the room and let him decide. Initially John picked his father, but then changed his mind and ran to his mother in tears. Freddie went back to sea, and vanished from John's life.

But having dispatched John's father, Julia discovered she had no use for a five-year-old. The boy was interfering with her affair with John Dykins, so Julia sent young John to live with his Aunt Mimi. Without divorcing Freddie, Julia moved in with Dykins and would eventually bear his children.

* * *

John's no-nonsense Aunt Mimi could not have stood in starker contrast to her sister. She and her husband, George Smith, ran their middle-class household with military precision. Mimi was hardly a picture of maternal love, but she provided John with stability, support and security.

Mimi and George lived in a middle-class, suburban

neighbourhood called Allerton. They named their mock Tudor house "Mendips" after its address on Menlove Avenue.

It was a new world for John. In his own words, Mendips was "a nice, semidetached place with a small garden and doctors and lawyers and that ilk living around – not the poor slummy kind of image that was projected in all the Beatles stories".

Uncle George ran a racetrack bookmaking operation from home and collected rents on some cottages he had inherited. Other than that, George did no work at all.

In this atmosphere of middle-class respectability, John was encouraged to act posh and read good books. He took to reading with a passion. The middle-class respectability was another story.

In spite of the stability Mimi provided, John exhibited behavioural problems. In the spring of 1946, at age five and a half, he was expelled from kindergarten for misbehaving. This expulsion set the pattern for his subsequent schooling. Bright and well-read, John was nevertheless a poor student who had great difficulty writing and spelling. A modern educator might have diagnosed John with dyslexia, but at the time, his teachers were convinced he was simply lazy.

As John's marks declined, so did his eyesight. To his horror, he was told he needed to wear glasses. Specs helped him see properly, but interfered with his burgeoning tough-guy reputation.

To Mimi's dismay, John became a wild child and a bully.

He blew up firecrackers in letterboxes, made prank phone calls and beat up weaker children. "The gang I led went in for shoplifting and pulling girls' knickers down", Lennon related to *Rolling Stone* magazine. "Other boys' parents hated me. Most of the [school] masters hated me".

In private, John continued to read, write and draw. Mimi encouraged his artistic side, seeing it as a sign of refinement. That didn't stop her from tossing out his poetry when it began piling up. John warned Mimi that he would be famous some day and she would regret her aggressive spring cleaning.

Indeed, John was convinced he was bound for future glory. "People like me are aware of their so-called genius at ten, eight, nine", John later stated. "I always wondered, 'why has nobody discovered me'?"

His genius remained undiscovered, even as he entered a new academic institution – Quarry Bank Grammar School – in September 1952. Quarry Bank closely resembled a prep school; students had to wear white shirts, black blazers and caps, and the school placed a high emphasis on academic achievement. Mimi hoped this rigorous environment would prod her surrogate son to work harder.

John, however, was none too enthusiastic about the dress code or the academic expectations. He was an indifferent student at Quarry Bank, scoring poor marks and disrupting classes.

While attending Quarry Bank, John divided his time between Mendips and the home of his birth mother. He would cut school in order to hang out with Julia during the day. Julia, who was happy to play hostess to John and his friends, encouraged this truancy. She rarely disciplined her son, and she treated his schooling like a joke.

John also got along well with Dykins, who liked him in return. Julia, for her part, had grown fonder of John now that he was older. She enjoyed putting on a show for him and his friends – singing merrily, playing boisterous tunes on the piano and acting like a showbiz diva.

Julia had two daughters courtesy of Dykins. Their names were Julie and Jacqueline and they were on reasonably good terms with their half-brother, John.

On 5 June 1955, Uncle George died at 52. Mimi was devastated, though she quickly recovered. For John, it was like his father disappearing all over again. He was now being raised almost entirely by women.

Shortly after Uncle George died, John discovered Elvis Presley. The former truck driver was setting America on fire with his good looks and raw talent. Elvis pioneered a new musical form called rock 'n' roll, and was an inspiration to millions of kids. John was fixated. He began dressing like a Teddy Boy.

Liverpool entered a steep decline after World War II. Unemployment was high and the city was becoming increasingly violent and dangerous. The Teddy Boys were part of a wide mix of jobless young people who enjoyed rock 'n' roll and rioting in equal measure.

Inspired by her son's newfound love of Elvis, Julia bought John a cheap acoustic guitar. John practised obsessively, to Mimi's dismay. Julia, who knew how to play the banjo, taught her son some finger patterns and chords. Mimi was not impressed. She insisted that he practise on the porch, where he wouldn't disturb her.

Fuelled by his passion for Elvis, and rockers such as Little Richard, John formed his first band. The group was called "The Quarry Men" after Quarry Bank School, and consisted of John and a clutch of friends. The Quarry Men didn't actually play rock 'n' roll, but rather "skiffle". Skiffle was essentially fast, driving folk music played on a guitar with rudimentary accompanying instruments such as washboards.

On 21 June 1957, John and the Quarry Men played their first concert. Wearing a checked shirt, his guitar strapped around his shoulder, John led his band through several skiffle tunes at a neighbourhood party. The Quarry Men did an adequate job but they were hardly impressive.

Two weeks after their debut gig, the band gave a daytime concert at a church fete. After their brief show was over, a dark-haired teenager in a white jacket and black trousers introduced himself to John. His name was Paul McCartney and he wasn't quite 16 years old.

Paul, who loved rock 'n' roll as much as John, praised the Quarry Men for their performance. Paul did take a moment to point out, however, that the band wasn't terribly professional. John tended to fake lyrics and couldn't actually play the guitar very well. A born showman, Paul picked up a guitar and performed an impromptu version of "Twenty Flight Rock" by Eddie Cochran and "Be-Bop-a-Lula" by Gene Vincent. Paul had an excellent voice, was a good guitar player and possessed a definite poise. A couple of weeks after their first introduction, John invited Paul to join his band.

Despite his reservations about the fledgling band's abilities, Paul jumped at the chance. He was attracted to the prospect of joining an already formed group – and he was drawn to John, with his obvious charisma and bad-boy attitude.

The two teens shared a couple of things in common. In addition to their love of music, John and Paul had each lost a parent. Freddie Lennon had been absent from John's life since he was a child while Paul's mother had died of cancer in 1956.

Other than that, Lennon and McCartney were as different as Elvis and Liberace. Unlike John, Paul had been raised in a stable, loving home. His father – who took on all the household responsibilities after his wife died – taught Paul to be thrifty, self-directed and disciplined. Paul was a natural charmer with a diplomatic personality. He carried none of John's bile and bitterness.

Being a talented musician, Paul thought it was his duty to teach his new friend how to play the guitar properly. Paul was left-handed, a fact that made lessons unusually complicated for the right-handed John, though it did contribute to a pleasing symmetry on stage.

For all their differences, John and Paul were soon jamming on a regular basis. The sounds they produced were crude, but enthusiastic. They played rock 'n' roll songs, skiffle tunes and anything else that caught their fancy.

In the fall of 1957, John enrolled in the Liverpool College of Art. He quickly dropped his Teddy Boy look in favour of a beatnik appearance. The beatnik movement had arisen in the United States as a reaction to the conservative materialism of the day. "Beats" liked to wear black clothing, listen to jazz music and mock middle-class values.

Once again, John was a poor student – and an excellent prankster. He enjoyed being the class clown, cracking up fellow students with jokes and cartoons. And while he paid little attention to his studies, he took his music far more seriously. He jammed continuously with Paul and a loose circle of other amateur musicians.

After a few months of playing together, Paul casually mentioned that he had a friend who was an even better guitarist than himself. The boy's name was George Harrison; he was shy, intense and almost three years younger than John. During his audition for the Quarry Men, George played a note-perfect version of an instrumental piece called "Raunchy". John was impressed and in early February 1958, George joined the fledgling band.

Paul and George attended the Liverpool Institute, which was conveniently located near the College of Art. The three young men frequently played guitar together during their lunch hours. George usually handled lead guitar while John and Paul played rhythm. John and Paul took turns singing vocals while George piped in on the chorus or sang backup. John had a raspy, tough-guy voice. Paul had a wider range, but generally sounded sweeter, whether he was singing rock 'n' roll or a pop ballad.

The boys' talents complemented each other, as did their personalities. While John was clearly the leader, Paul was the band's showman – eager to ham it up to draw attention from the girls. John brought a raw rocker sensibility to the group while studious George provided a strong musical foundation. Everything pointed to rapidly rising success – until the band was sidetracked by tragedy.

In the summer of 1958, a speeding driver killed Julia Lennon as she walked across the street. In later years, Lennon described Julia's death as "the worst-ever thing that happened to me".

After going to the hospital to view his dead mother, John went into shock. His neighbours saw him playing his guitar on his front porch, a lost, devastated young man. Music was his only solace. He played for hours, trying to bury his pain in rock riffs.

Julia's death ignited John's already malicious sense of humour. He began to lash out at the handicapped, the elderly and other defenseless souls. As he wandered around Liverpool, anyone who attracted his attention might set him off, drawing raging torrents of verbal abuse.

Though he was devastated by Julia's death, John continued to attend art school. He became extremely close to two students at the college: an intense young artist named Stuart Sutcliffe, and a shy, attractive girl named Cynthia Powell.

A proper, middle-class student, Cynthia had a huge crush on the College of Art's leading bad boy. Lennon soon returned her affections. One day, he invited her to join him at a pub. Afterwards, they repaired to a friend's flat and made love, still on their first date.

The flat in question belonged to Stuart Sutcliffe. Handsome Sutcliffe cultivated a James Dean-like image – moody, sensitive and brilliant. He had a reputation as one of the college's most promising students.

Just as Cynthia became John's unlikely girlfriend, Stu became his mismatched best friend. In early 1960, John moved into Sutcliffe's flat, which was cluttered with paintings and art equipment.

Shortly after John moved in with him, Stuart won £65 in an art show – a large sum at the time. John convinced him to spend his winnings on a Hohner electric bass guitar. Stuart did as his friend suggested, and started playing bass in John's group.

By this point, the Quarry Men had long since disbanded. John, Paul and George had graduated to electric guitars and had given up skiffle in favour of fast, raw rock 'n' roll.

Stuart lacked any sense of musical talent, but he made up for it in other ways. He looked good and had great stage presence. More substantively, he suggested that John's group called themselves "The Beetles" after the name of a gang in the motorcycle film, *The Wild One.* Lennon changed the tag to "Beatles" – a pun on "beats all" and "beat" music.

With a series of temporary drummers, the fledgling Beatles began rehearsing and performing around Liverpool.

The band often practised at a dingy coffee house located in the Liverpool 8 – a seedy, bohemian district. The coffee shop was called the Jacaranda ("the Jac" in local parlance) and was run by a short, energetic hustler named Allan Williams. Williams was friends with Stuart Sutcliffe, who introduced the club owner to the rest of the Beatles.

Williams liked having music in the basement of the Jac. He had two house bands: a gang of West Indian steel drummers, and a tight, fast rock group called Cass and the Casanovas. Williams didn't deem the Beatles good enough to serve as a headlining act, so he used them as a "lull" band, filling in slow moments at the coffee shop. In return for their amateur services, Williams provided the Beatles with free coffee and greasy bacon sandwiches.

At the time, the Beatles' "uniform" consisted of black sweaters, black jeans and trainers. The boys had greasy hair and looked more like a pack of street kids than a proper rock 'n' roll group. In spite of their ratty appearance, Williams decided to become the Beatles part-time manager in May 1960.

That same month, Williams hosted a series of auditions for Larry Parnes, a big-time music promoter from London who was looking to hire a back-up band for one of his stars, Billy Fury. With a stand-in drummer, the Beatles performed a knockout audition. Parnes, however, noticed right away that Sutcliffe couldn't actually play. Stu was so untalented, he let his fingers roam around the neck of his bass at random in an unconvincing imitation of music.

Billy Fury was eager to hire the Beatles but Parnes was adamant – if Sutcliffe stayed, the band wouldn't get the gig. Parnes asked the Beatles to audition without Stu, but they refused.

A few days later, Parnes hired the Beatles anyway, to back up a lesser star in his stable named Johnny Gentle. Gentle, who was never a chart-topping performer, was about to embark on a tour of Scotland. The Beatles acquired a temporary drummer named Tommy Moore and drove to Scotland in a van with Gentle. They were ecstatic – the Scotland tour would be their first real, professional touring gig. For Lennon, the opportunity came not a moment too soon. He was failing at art college, largely due to lack of effort. If he failed at rock 'n' roll, his career options in rough and tumble Liverpool looked bleak at best.

Chapter 2
Love Me Do

There was little show-business glamour to be found on the Beatles' first professional tour. Their shows with Johnny Gentle were held before sullen Scottish teenagers in low-rent ballrooms and dance halls. The tour itself was mercifully short – seven towns in nine days.

The routine at each show was the same: the Beatles would come out and play a few rock 'n' roll numbers to warm up the crowd. Then Johnny Gentle would take centre stage and sing a handful of songs as the Beatles backed him up. After that, Johnny would disappear and the Beatles would close the show with a few more tunes.

The Beatles were being paid almost nothing for their efforts and were forced to travel around Scotland in a cramped, old van. Making things worse, the organiser of the tour refused to pay Stu Sutcliffe a penny. Larry Parnes thought that only real musicians deserved wages. The Beatles had to pool their already meagre salaries in order to buy food for Stu.

At one point, the touring van got into an accident. No one inside was hurt, except for drummer Tommy Moore, who got smacked in the face by a guitar case. He lost his front teeth and was taken to a local hospital for stitches. Moore was still at the hospital when the remaining Beatles showed up for their gig.

The concert promoter was none too pleased to see that the band lacked a drummer. The boys told him about the accident, but the promoter wasn't mollified. Foolishly, Lennon thought he'd have a bit of fun with the man. Lennon suggested that if the promoter was so keen on having a drummer, why didn't he just go to the hospital and drag Tommy to the show?

Unfortunately for Moore, the promoter did just that. He drove to the hospital and literally grabbed Moore out of bed. Still groggy from the anaesthetic, Moore somehow managed to play that evening.

Far from being impressed by Moore's perseverance, Lennon laughed and made jokes about Moore's appearance. Not surprisingly, Moore quit the band after the Scottish tour wrapped up. He went back to his job in a bottling factory and refused to have anything more to do with the Beatles.

Drummer aside, the Scottish tour proved to be a huge boon for the Beatles. Their playing and singing improved enormously on tour. The pressure of having to perform night after night to disinterested audiences had turned them into crack entertainers. Once they got back to Liverpool, the Beatles began to garner a reputation as one of the hottest live acts in a city that was tailor made for rock 'n' roll.

Liverpool was a port city and very cosmopolitan. Sailors brought in new records purchased during their travels, exposing local youths to sounds from around the world. But it was also a poor city. Teenagers couldn't afford to attend expensive shows at swanky ballrooms, as they did in other British cities. As a result, they formed their own bands and entertained each other. Kids who weren't in bands went to see their friends and acquaintances play.

Promoters quickly realised that they could make handsome profits in the music business. They could hire a slew of teen bands for poverty-level wages, rent a cheap hall and some primitive sound equipment for next to nothing, then make a killing selling tickets.

Fuelled by cheap talent, the Liverpool scene burgeoned to over 300 bands, as well as a homegrown music paper called *Mersey Beat* (an appropriate name, as Liverpool drummers took a sledgehammer approach to keeping time, brutally slamming their sticks against the snare drum).

With so many musicians playing around town, the Beatles managed to snag a new drummer relatively quickly.

His name was Pete Best and he was handsome and moody. Most importantly, he owned his own drum kit. Best's mother ran a teen club called the Casbah in the basement of her expansive home.

Pete wasn't particularly talented or personable, but he would do. Besides, Lennon reasoned, his good looks would help the band attract female followers.

Shortly after Pete Best assumed the drummer's chair, the Beatles caught another lucky break. In the summer of 1960, Allan Williams's West Indian steel band was offered a better-paying gig in Hamburg, Germany – another port city packed with clubs offering all manner of entertainment.

Sensing an opportunity, Williams hooked up with a German club owner named Bruno Koshmider. A former circus performer, Koshmider wanted to hire British rock groups to perform in Hamburg's red-light district, the Reeperbahn. The promoter didn't think that German bands could play rock 'n' roll properly.

Williams arranged for some Liverpool groups to perform at Koshmider's club. The Beatles pestered him until they too got the nod to play in Hamburg.

In mid-August 1960, the five Beatles – John, Paul, George, Stu and Pete – took a ferry to Hamburg, where they were booked to perform at Club Indra. The Indra was a former striptease bar and the Beatles – fully clothed and lacking curves – did not go over well; the crowds wanted naked women, not English musicians. The few patrons who liked the Beatles' music were bored by their performance. German audiences expected rock bands to jump around on stage and act crazy. Crowds at Club Indra shouted "*Mach Schau! Mach Schau!*" (Make show!)

The Beatles hadn't previously given much thought to their stage act. Usually, they just stood in place and played. To appease the demanding Germans, they began revving it up. As usual, Lennon led the charge. He started offering Nazi salutes from stage and taunted the audience with memories of World War II. He wore a toilet seat around his neck and pranced about the stage like a madman. The rest of the Beatles followed suit, pounding their boots against the flimsy stage to keep time.

The intoxicated crowds at Club Indra loved it. They egged the Beatles on to be even more outrageous. Often, anonymous crowd members deposited cases of free booze on stage for the band to consume, hoping to add fuel to their fiery performances. It worked.

The Beatles' gig at Club Indra only lasted for seven weeks. Koshmider was forced to close the club due to noise complaints, but he didn't want to lose the Beatles so he quickly got them another gig at a Hamburg club called the Kaiserkeller. The Kaiserkeller was a bigger venue with a red-hot house band called Rory Storm and the Hurricanes. A top-notch Liverpool live act, the Hurricanes featured a flashily attired drummer named Ringo Starr. As his name implied, Ringo wore a series of rings on his fingers. It set him apart, as did his long, greasy hair and scraggly beard. At the Kaiserkeller, the Beatles alternated shows with Rory Storm. Just like at Club Indra, the Beatles were contracted to play incredibly long sets. Sometimes, they would be on stage from dusk to dawn, performing for seven or eight hours.

"In Liverpool, we'd only ever done one-hour sessions and we just used to do our best numbers, the same ones, at every one", Lennon stated years later. "In Hamburg, we had to play for eight hours, so we had to find a new way of playing. We played very loud! Bang! Bang! All the time".

In addition to playing loud, the Beatles began stretching their material out. A 2-minute pop song might turn into a 15-minute epic. As Lennon observed, audiences didn't seem to mind. Indeed, the German crowds stomped and screamed whenever the band went into a lengthy jam.

For their appearances in Germany, the Beatles had taken to wearing black leather pants and jackets and motorcycle boots. It was the same uniform that most audience members wore.

While the Beatles might have *looked* like hoodlums, Kaiserkeller patrons were the real thing. They were constantly starting fights with each other. The instant a brawl broke out, beefy bouncers rushed to break it up, or at least, toss the offenders outside. Flying beer mugs and random punches were an occupational hazard for the bands that performed at the club.

In Hamburg, the Beatles had to make do with extremely

poor living quarters. They were housed in a warren of dirty rooms located behind the screen of a movie theatre. These dingy rooms witnessed a great deal of partying and womanising. To stay awake for their marathon concerts, the band began to take "Prellies" (Preludin, a kind of amphetamine).

When the band wasn't playing or partying, they listened to other English groups performing in Hamburg. They were friendly with most of the British bands, especially Rory Storm and the Hurricanes. The Beatles particularly liked Rory's drummer, Ringo. Ringo was humble, had a great sense of humour and was eager to please – traits that John appreciated in other men. Ringo and the Beatles were soon fast friends.

* * *

The Beatles continued to commute back and forth between Liverpool and Hamburg, gradually building up followings in both cities.

Despite the constant travel, John remained close to his Liverpool friends and family. He kept Cynthia Powell as his girlfriend – while cheating on her constantly – and stayed at Aunt Mimi's house whenever he was in town.

In February 1961, the Beatles played their first lunch date at a Liverpool club called the Cavern. Located in the basement of an old warehouse, the Cavern consisted of 3 parallel tunnels, each 3 metres wide and 30 metres long. In the central tunnel were 20 narrow rows of wooden chairs facing a low stage on which bands played.

When the Cavern was crowded, the walls literally dripped with condensation. Ventilation was non-existent and the air reeked of sweat, perfume and cigarette smoke. The acoustics, of course, were dreadful.

Despite its raw amenities, the Cavern became the "in" spot in Liverpool for concerts. And the Beatles became a house favourite.

In the spring of 1961, the band left Liverpool for another engagement in Hamburg. Their new residency was not at the Kaiserkeller, but at a competing establishment called the Top Ten Club.

While the Top Ten Club was a big step up, the residency caused a permanent break between the Beatles and Allan Williams. Williams felt he had helped get the Beatles the Top Ten gig, and was entitled to a percentage of their fee. The Beatles claimed they got the gig themselves and refused to pay. When he realised that no money would be forthcoming, Williams angrily severed his ties with the band.

Not long after the Beatles started their Top Ten residency, Stu quit the group. He did so after considerable lobbying from Paul, who was frustrated with Stu's musical incompetence. He may also have been jealous of Stu's good looks and his close relationship with John, who was clearly the leader of the band.

Stu's official explanation for quitting the Beatles was to be with his new girlfriend, a beautiful Hamburg girl called

Astrid Kircherr. Astrid was an "Exi" – a German university student who affected a bohemian, existential air and an artistic manner.

The Exis were neatly dressed, intellectually minded, and big fans of the Beatles. Male Exis wore their hair like schoolboys, with a long fringe swept across their forehead. They stood out amidst the leather-clad audiences at the Kaiserkeller.

Stu, too, stopped greasing his hair and began combing it across his forehead. The other Beatles copied the look, which gave them a distinctive, floppy haired appearance.

Exiled from the Beatles, Stu nevertheless continued to exert significant influence on John. The pair would hang out when the Beatles played in Hamburg and exchange lengthy letters when they weren't. Stu had taken up painting once again and was concentrating on his art – at which he displayed real talent. Stu threw himself into his painting with such intensity that John feared for his health – particularly when his friend complained of fierce headaches.

Though he missed Stu, John had to admit the Beatles sounded much better without him. In Stu's absence, Paul took up bass duties. He proved to be a master of the instrument, anchoring the Beatles' tunes with solid bass lines.

The new, more professional sounding Beatles made their first record in June 1961. They piled into a cramped Hamburg studio and laid down background music for a singer named Tony Sheridan. With the Beatles backing him, Tony belted out a series of traditional tunes, including

"My Bonnie" and "When the Saints Go Marching In".

The songs they recorded sounded flat and tinny, but the Beatles were pleased. Perhaps the recordings would gain them a few new fans in Hamburg and Liverpool.

* * *

Throughout the fall of 1961, teenagers poured into the NEMS record store in Liverpool requesting "My Bonnie" by Tony Sheridan. The high demand for the record caught the attention of store manager Brian Epstein.

At 27 years old, Epstein was neatly dressed and well mannered. He came from a wealthy Jewish merchant family, but had endured a troubled youth. Gay and insecure, he had been kicked out of several schools. He longed to be an actor but had dropped out of drama school before graduating.

If he was a bad actor, Epstein was an excellent record store manager. He took customer requests seriously and did his best to stock even the most obscure records.

Epstein ordered several copies of "My Bonnie" and was pleased to see how fast they sold. He was surprised to discover that the Beatles were a Liverpool act; the single was recorded in Hamburg, so Epstein had assumed the band was German.

Something about the Beatles piqued his curiosity. After learning that the band was playing a series of lunchtime concerts at the Cavern, he resolved to see the group live. On

9 November 1961, he descended into the murky depths of the Cavern to catch a typically raucous Beatles show.

Epstein was impressed by the Beatles' sound, but didn't think much of their stage act. The band smoked, drank and ate during their performance and got into arguments about what song to play next. They spent as much time messing around as they did playing music.

If their stage manners left something to be desired, Epstein noted the wild reaction the Beatles inspired in their fans. Even at a lunchtime concert, the Cavern was packed. After the set was over, Epstein introduced himself to the Beatles. His initial meeting was purely exploratory. He wanted to meet the band who had such a devoted following.

Epstein began to harbour notions of becoming the Beatles' manager. The thought was highly appealing for a failed actor who appreciated the Beatles' youthful spirit and irreverent wit. Some in the music business believed that Epstein had more than just monetary gain in mind; rumour had it that he fancied John.

It didn't bother Epstein that he had never managed a rock group before. He was convinced that with hustle and polish he could make the band famous.

The Beatles, for their part, were highly receptive to Epstein's pitch. They worried they might be stuck playing in Hamburg and Liverpool forever.

Despite a warning from Allan Williams (who told the record store manager that he wouldn't touch the Beatles with a barge pole) Epstein took over management of the band in late 1961.

One of Epstein's first duties involved easing Aunt Mimi's fears. Mimi wanted John to give up rock 'n' roll and finish his interrupted studies at art school. She made Epstein promise to take special care of John. It was a request Epstein readily agreed to.

Next, Epstein decided to clean the Beatles up. He encouraged them to wear suits and ties instead of leather and forbade them from eating, drinking or smoking on stage. Set lists were adhered to and the band no longer played tunes at random.

After polishing their image, Epstein went about promoting the group to record labels. On 1 January 1962, the Beatles had an audition with Decca records in London. They played 15 songs, but Decca wasn't impressed. According to legend, a Decca executive said, "We don't like their sound. Groups of guitars are on their way out".

* * *

Having failed to find an interested record label, the Beatles returned to Hamburg on April 11. This time, they went in style – on a jet, not a dirty ferry. The band had been contracted to perform at a high profile venue called the Star Club.

John had planned to meet Stu and Astrid at Hamburg airport. He hoped to catch up with the pair before the Beatles took the stage. Stu didn't show up. Astrid met him alone, and she was red-faced from crying. Stu, she told John, was dead. He had died only the day before, of a brain hemorrhage. The headaches Stu had complained of were symptoms of a brain tumour that had gone undiagnosed.

John stood in the airport terminal, reeling with shock from Astrid's news. Another person close to him had died unexpectedly. He wondered if he was under a curse that condemned everyone who grew close to him to death.

The Beatles didn't have long to mourn. They took the stage only hours after receiving Astrid's staggering news. The band mates tore into a fiery set of rock 'n' roll and pop standards to a boisterous audience. The band blew the roof off the Star Club that night, amazing the crowd and solidifying their reputation as the hottest live act in both Britain and Germany.

* * *

While the Beatles played out their residency at the Star Club, Epstein – who by now was the band's official manager – scurried about trying to land a record deal in Britain. After being turned down countless times by smug record executives, he finally managed to land a contract in the spring of 1962. The interested party was one George Martin, a producer at Parlophone (a division of EMI). According to Brian Epstein, Martin resembled "a stern but fair-minded housemaster".

Cool, calm and unfailingly polite, Martin was a respected but largely obscure producer. While not enormously impressed by the Beatles' sound, he did like their vocal arrangements and the fact that each member of the band sang, which was unusual in the early 1960s.

In later years, Martin would admit there was one other reason he signed the Beatles: at the time, Columbia Records had a singer named Cliff Richards under contract. Richards was considered a hot property in the British music scene. Martin was eager to find a pop act of his own who could compete with Richards in the charts. He figured the Beatles might do, with a bit of studio polishing, of course.

So it was that on 6 June 1962, the Beatles stood about nervously in the cramped confines of the EMI studios on Abbey Road in London, running through an abbreviated set for George Martin. The band had signed with EMI only two days earlier. Now, they were performing live in the studio for Martin to give him a better idea of their sound.

By this point, John and Paul were writing their own material. They had emerged as the chief songwriters in the group, although their early compositions weren't very memorable. Martin thought their tunes were okay, but he insisted they change drummers. Pete Best was weak, said Martin. He would have to be replaced by a studio drummer when it came time to record.

It was music to the other Beatles ears; as with Stu, McCartney resented their drummer's good looks and the attention he drew from the girls. Lennon found Best overconfident and impossible to boss around. They ordered Epstein to fire their drummer.

The remaining Beatles already had a replacement in mind: their buddy Ringo Starr, formerly of Rory Storm and the Hurricanes. To become one of the Beatles, Ringo was told to shave his beard and arrange his hair into a "mop top" – directives with which he meekly complied.

The band took to Ringo immediately, though neither their fans nor George Martin were as easily convinced. Martin was astonished to discover that Ringo hadn't even mastered basic percussive techniques, such as a drum roll. Fans – especially girls – missed Best. They would boo Ringo at every opportunity and wave signs with slogans like "Pete Forever Ringo Never".

But for all Ringo's inability on the drums he had a singular virtue: likeability. Always easygoing and quick with a joke, Ringo was soon embraced by fans, and Pete Best was forgotten.

In early September 1962, John, Paul, George and Ringo had their first proper recording session at Abbey Road. They decided to record one of their own compositions. Entitled "Love Me Do", it was a pleasant, if plodding pop tune that featured John on harmonica.

"Love Me Do" was released in October as the Beatles' debut single. It hit number 17 on the pop charts, and never rose any higher. Later that year, the Beatles conducted another recording session. This time, they recorded a much catchier Lennon and McCartney tune called "Please, Please Me". The song was fast and snappy and again featured John's bluesy harmonica. For the first time, the Beatles managed to impress their stern producer. "Gentlemen", announced George Martin at the end of the session, "you've just made your first number one record".

* * *

While the Beatles were hitting their stride in the studio, Lennon was facing a personal crisis. Late that summer, his longtime girlfriend, Cynthia Powell, announced she was pregnant. Shocked, John concluded they had to get married.

Neither Aunt Mimi nor Epstein was pleased. Aunt Mimi felt John was too immature and that he clearly didn't love Cynthia. Epstein was worried that female fans might be put off if they found out Lennon was married.

Despite his misgivings, Epstein served as Lennon's best man at the service at a Liverpool municipal office on 23 August. Paul and George also attended, looking nervous and uptight.

The wedding was marred by the sound of a workman whose drilling made the ceremony inaudible. Following the ceremony, the Beatles repaired to a nearby restaurant that lacked a liquor license. Epstein toasted the unhappy groom and apprehensive bride with water. He later arranged for

Cynthia to stay at Mendips and instructed her to keep quiet about her nuptials.

Cynthia's treatment was a far cry from the tender sentiments expressed in "Love Me Do" and "Please, Please Me".

Chapter 3
Ticket to Ride

Over the course of one manic day in February 1963, the Beatles laid down all of the tracks for their first album. EMI wanted to spend as little as possible on their new catch, forcing the band to perform at a blitzkrieg pace.

Lennon and McCartney wrote most of the songs on the Beatles' debut album. Their styles meshed. John liked rock 'n' roll while Paul preferred sweet ballads. John wrote great lyrics while Paul excelled at melodies. Together, they crafted perfect pop tunes.

A few days after the marathon recording session at Abbey Road, the Beatles' second single, "Please, Please Me", topped the British music charts. George Martin's prediction had come true.

In March, the band released the album, which was also called *Please, Please Me*. It, too, was an instant hit.

Amidst all this excitement, Lennon's first child was born. He was named Julian and arrived on 8 April 1963.

Lennon did not instinctively take to fatherhood. In fact, he waited several days before seeing his new son. He briefly popped into the hospital to visit Cynthia and Julian, only to announce that he was going on vacation to Spain with Brian Epstein. This reduced Cynthia to tears, but even her sobs couldn't change John's travel plans.

Once she was released from hospital, Cynthia retreated to her mother's house. Cynthia and her new baby stayed there for a few months before being put up in a flat in London by Brian Epstein. Epstein was eager to keep Cynthia and Julian out of the media spotlight. In practise, this meant keeping mother and son far away from John.

If Lennon felt uneasy being a father, he was equally uncomfortable with his new musical persona. Epstein had smoothed out the Beatles' rebellious edges. The Beatles now wore collarless jackets on stage and were polite and mannerly at all times. Their once wild, greasy hair was now neatly combed in a schoolboy style. They no longer guzzled beer and popped Prellies – at least not on stage.

To John, all these changes reeked of selling out. Where he had once been a wild young rocker, he was now a tame family entertainer.

During their trip to Spain, John voiced his concerns

to Brian. The two had become quite close. While only a few years older than John, Epstein served as a surrogate father figure for the young pop star. For his part, Brian clearly admired – and possibly desired – the leader of the Beatles.

As far as Epstein was concerned, cleaning up the Beatles image made good business sense. Certainly, the band was a lot more popular because of it. Still, Lennon wasn't satisfied with Brian's reassurances. As the Beatles breakthrough year continued, he continued to look warily upon life as a superstar, husband and father.

* * *

On the evening of 13 October 1963, the Beatles completed their rise from popular regional act to national sensation. The occasion was a television variety show called *Val Parnell's Sunday Night at the London Palladium.*

The street outside the London building where the TV show was broadcast was packed with some 2,000 girls. They cried hysterically and screamed out the names of John, Paul, George and Ringo, over and over. When the band emerged after the show, the girls swarmed past a line of policemen and charged at the four shaggy-haired young men. The Beatles dived into a waiting Austin Princess car and raced off, leaving a mob of shrieking teenagers in their wake.

The band had been building momentum all year, releasing a string of hits and playing sold-out shows across the country. Their latest single was called "She Loves You" and had a simple, catchy chorus that went, "yeah, yeah, yeah".

The press took note of the pandemonium at the Palladium show. One reporter even came up with a special word to describe the frenzy: "Beatlemania". It spread like a virus.

In early November 1963, the band played a Royal Variety Show at London's Prince of Wales Theatre. Among those in attendance were the Queen Mother and Princess Margaret. In front of these royals, Lennon offered a cheeky quip. "Those of you in the cheaper seats, clap your hands", instructed John. "And those of you in the more expensive seats, just rattle your jewellery".

The audience exploded with laughter as the Beatles launched into their next number. John's remarks helped cement his reputation as the comedian of the band. In fact, all four Beatles had a sparkling, irreverent sense of humour. On top of their music, the Beatles were becoming famous for their wit – and their increasingly long hair.

Later in November, the Beatles released their biggest hit to date, "I Want to Hold Your Hand". It shot to the top of the charts and stayed there for five weeks. While delighted, the Beatles knew they had one more market to conquer. So far, their records had flopped in the United States, the birthplace of rock 'n' roll. The band hoped that "I Want to Hold Your Hand" might do better than its predecessors among American record buyers.

In mid-January 1964, the Beatles played a three-week

engagement in France. Audiences there didn't appear to get the Beatles. They sat on their hands for the most part and regarded the boys with near contempt.

The Beatles soon recovered from their less than successful reception. During a dinner in Paris, a phone call came through for Brian Epstein. Epstein took the call, then returned to the table, looking dazed and delighted. The four Beatles gaped at their usually cool manager, wondering what had set him in such a strange mood.

When he caught his breath, Epstein made an incredible announcement. "I Want To Hold Your Hand", said the Beatles manager, was the number one song in the United States. The Beatles were ready to invade America.

* * *

The Fab Four – as they were now affectionately called – made a triumphant entry to North America on 7 February 1964. Roughly 3,000 screaming fans showed up at JFK airport in New York City to greet them.

"I Want To Hold Your Hand" had sold two million copies in America, without the Beatles performing a note in the country. Radio stations were playing a continuous stream of Beatles tunes while newspapers and television crews followed the band's every move.

The Beatles' first North American press conference was held in the terminal of JFK airport. A total of 200 reporters showed up for the event, peppering the band with qucstions.

"What do you do when you're cooped up in your rooms?" demanded a reporter.

"We ice skate", replied Harrison.

"Was your family in show business?" a journalist asked John.

"Well, me dad used to say me mother was a great performer", replied Lennon, with a leer.

The reporters laughed and the Beatles were whisked away to prepare for their American debut. Brian had arranged for the band to perform live on *The Ed Sullivan Show,* one of the highest-rated TV programmes in the United States. If all went according to plan, the Beatles' performance would be viewed by millions of people.

The Ed Sullivan Show went off without a hitch on 9 February. With their distinctive suits and ties, and now collar-length pudding bowl hair, the Beatles appearance caused a sensation. An estimated 73 million viewers – then the largest television audience in history – tuned in for the Beatles' masterful performance.

Paul sang lead on five of the six numbers the Beatles played. Brian wanted to emphasise the band's softer material, which generally featured McCartney's sweet vocals. John wasn't pleased, but went along with the arrangement.

At the end of their set, the Fab Four bowed to their audience. It was a neat touch. By looking humble, the band managed to win over even their stodgiest critics.

On 11 February, two days after performing on *The Ed Sullivan Show*, the Beatles played their first real concert in the U.S. The gig was held in Washington, D.C., in front of 20,000 screaming youngsters. This was a far larger crowd than they were used to in Europe, where concert venues were much smaller.

The enormous audience made it impossible to hear anything. The band's tiny 50-watt guitar amplifiers were easily drowned out by the raucous screams of their fans.

By the time the Beatles played Washington, D.C., they had almost totally taken over the American pop charts. During one frenzied week in April 1964, the Beatles occupied the top five spots on the U.S. singles chart. This was a feat no band had ever achieved before. The songs in question were "Can't Buy Me Love", "Twist and Shout", "She Loves You", "I Want to Hold Your Hand" and "Please, Please Me".

The Beatles' incredible reception in America had a lot to do with timing. By 1964, the first wave of American rock 'n' rollers had largely vanished. Elvis Presley had gone into the army and returned a tamed, non-threatening crooner. Buddy Holly was dead, Little Richard had joined the church, and Chuck Berry and Jerry Lee Lewis had both been disgraced by sex scandals.

The Beatles also provided a bit of cheer in an otherwise dismal time in American history. Only four months before the Fab Four played *The Ed Sullivan Show*, popular young president John F. Kennedy had been assassinated. The Beatles were the perfect antidote to the national mood of mourning. Their music was cheerful and catchy, their manner loveable.

The Beatles had hit on a winning formula that was soon to be copied by countless groups. They blended high-energy rock music with sweet group-vocal harmonies. Unlike most rock bands of the era, which consisted of a flashy front man and anonymous backup musicians, the Beatles comprised four distinct individuals. Paul was seen as cute and charming, Ringo was loveable and dumb and George was serious and mysterious. John was the "smart Beatle", always quick with a quip.

In March 1964, John cemented that reputation with the release of his first book. Called *In His Own Write*, it consisted of John's Lewis-Carroll inspired nonsense writing. His silly scribblings became an instant hit. *In His Own Write* sold 100,000 copies in its first printing, making John a bestselling author.

As ever, John's professional success couldn't insulate him from the chaos of his family life. A month after his publishing triumph, Lennon received a surprising and not entirely welcome visitor – his father, Freddie.

Despite nearly 20 years apart, Freddie was eerily familiar to John. The two had similar facial features, and even Freddie's voice and sense of humour were the same as John's.

Unlike the leader of the Beatles, however, Freddie Lennon wasn't much to look at; his hair was long and greasy, he was missing most of his teeth and his face showed the effects of hard living.

While John didn't know it, and Freddie didn't mention it, the elder Lennon had tried to get in touch with his son after leaving him at Blackpool. In 1949, he had returned to England from a stint at sea determined to rescue John from the clutches of his birth mother. Unfortunately, Freddie had decided to get drunk before visiting John. Intoxicated, he had smashed a store window and was promptly arrested. As a result, Freddie had lost his seaman's papers and wasn't allowed to work on ships anymore. He became homeless and drifted about the country, earning his keep by doing menial labour, such as washing dishes.

Freddie was still doing such menial jobs, even as his son rose to the top of the pop music world. John felt sorry for his dad, but he also felt disgust at the man's terrible appearance and pathetic existence. He made a note not to invite his father back for any future family reunions.

* * *

As Freddie returned to the squalid world of cheap hotels and lousy jobs, John went about trying to find himself a house. In July 1964, he purchased a huge mock Tudor home called Kenwood in a wealthy suburb south of London.

John moved Cynthia and Julian into the house, then went on a month-long remodelling spree. He added his own peculiar touches to the home. In one room, Lennon set up a suit of armour topped with a gorilla's head. He placed a colour TV in the fireplace and kept it on perpetually, albeit without sound.

Shortly after John took up residence at Kenwood, the Beatles released their first movie, filmed earlier that year. Originally conceived as a quick knock-off, the movie was nevertheless surprisingly witty and entertaining. Entitled *A Hard Day's Night*, it featured a solid script and lots of good music.

The movie consisted of the Beatles' various misadventures in London. A sub-plot centred on the conflict between Paul and his fictional grandfather – a grouchy old man forever trying to profit at the Beatles' expense.

The music in the film was fantastic. The title song alone became an instant classic. As sung by John, it featured highly original 12-string electric guitar work from George. Few pop bands had ever used 12-string guitars on a recording. Once again, the Beatles were setting the pace for pop music.

A Hard Day's Night got good reviews. *The Village Voice* in New York City described it as the "Citizen Kane of jukebox musicals". It played in hundreds of American theatres and proved the Beatles were capable of dominating yet another medium.

In late summer 1964, the Beatles embarked on their first tour of North America. Between 19 August and 20 September 1964, the Fab Four played 32 shows in two-dozen cities.

For the duration of the tour, the band mates were essentially prisoners in their fancy hotel suites. They couldn't even walk the hallways without drawing hordes of howling, crying girls. As a result, the Beatles spent most of their time in isolation, downing their favourite drink, Scotch and coke. If the booze affected their performance, it hardly mattered; their concerts lasted less than an hour and were almost completely drowned out by the shrieks of the crowd.

The Beatles did enjoy one epochal moment during the first North American tour, with superstar folk singer Bob Dylan. In the course of the meeting, Dylan offered the lads some marijuana he happened to have on him. The Beatles confessed they had never smoked grass before, although they were willing to try. They discovered they liked the gentle buzz quite a bit. Soon they were smoking the drug all the time.

Whether it was the drugs, or simply the result of his maturing songwriting ability, John's compositions began to take on a personal, much more introspective flavour. In early 1965, he produced an excellent, driving rock 'n' roll tune with acutely sensitive lyrics. Entitled "Help!", the song encapsulated John's emotions at the time.

The fast-paced rock tune was a hit in both Europe and America – though ironically, neither fans nor the other Beatles seemed to catch on to its true meaning. Touring took its toll on John. A daily regimen of fast food, booze and confinement left him out of shape and overweight, and the isolation was a drag on his spirits. By the end of the most successful tour in the band's history, Lennon felt distant and lost.

Chapter 4
Here, There and Everywhere

In mid-1965, the Beatles returned to North America bigger stars than ever. For their summer tour, the Fab Four performed almost exclusively in baseball stadiums – the largest venues available for pop concerts.

Playing such huge venues was Epstein's idea. Other managers thought he was crazy, but the Beatles drew sell-out crowds to every show. Fifty-five thousand fans watched the Beatles perform at New York City's Shea Stadium. It was the biggest audience ever gathered in one spot for a rock 'n' roll concert. Film cameras captured every moment.

Just like the year before, the Beatles' concerts were extremely short, sometimes lasting only 20 minutes. The band couldn't put up with the nerve-wracking screams of their fans for much longer than that.

This was unfortunate, because the Beatles' musical output was growing apace. Monster hits such as "Eight Days a Week", "Ticket To Ride", "Yesterday" and "Day Tripper" were all released in 1965. The band's music and lyrical concerns were getting increasingly sophisticated.

A slew of British bands that had followed in the Beatles' wake were now scoring big chart hits in the United States. These groups included the Rolling Stones, the Kinks, Gerry and the Pacemakers and the Animals. The American press called it "The British Invasion". The invasion inspired countless teenagers to grow their hair long and form bands.

During their 1965 tour, the Beatles made a pilgrimage to a Bel Air mansion in California to meet one of their heroes, Elvis Presley. It was an inauspicious meeting from the start; Elvis, whose career had been in decline for some time, had retired from the concert stage, preferring the seclusion of his mansion.

Nonetheless, the Beatles still regarded him as a demigod. They crowded around Elvis in his Bel Air home and gazed at him in silent awe. Several moments passed in which no one spoke. The King finally broke the silence. "Look, guys", he said, "if you're just going to sit there and stare at me, I'm going to bed".

The Beatles took the hint but the conversation didn't go well. John asked Elvis if he was planning on recording some new tunes that contained the same fire and passion as his work from the 1950s. Presley took it as an insult. He thought John was implying that his new material wasn't any good. It wasn't – but Elvis didn't care for the truth.

Having failed at small talk, the five musicians pulled out their instruments and jammed for a while. The music helped break the ice, and the visit lasted for a couple of hours, but Lennon left the King's mansion in a deep funk. He thought Elvis was out of it and had lost touch with the contemporary music scene. In John's view, the King acted more like a spoiled rich kid than a rock 'n' roll rebel.

Actually, John had more in common with Elvis than he was willing to admit. After the 1965 tour ended, John retreated to Kenwood and spent his days sleeping and eating. Left to his own devices, he typically slept in until early afternoon, and then lay on a sofa reading newspapers and magazines. In a profile written during this period, British journalist Maureen Cleave referred to John as "the laziest person in England".

Ringo had a home nearby and John occasionally dropped by. Otherwise, he didn't socialise with the rest of the band. Here was another irony: fans assumed that John and Paul were best friends. In fact, they travelled in different circles. Paul enjoyed going to clubs and mixing with celebrities. John preferred to stay at home and relax.

If he avoided the Beatles, John was equally indifferent to his family. He tried to be a good father to Julian but got easily annoyed by the young toddler. Once annoyed, John would order Julian out of the room. Lennon paid even less attention to his sweet, meek wife Cynthia, who accepted her lowly status with stoic resolve.

Cynthia was so lonely that she had her mother, Lillian, move into Kenwood. John wasn't happy to see Mrs. Powell in his house. Cynthia's mother regarded John as a lazy good-for-nothing who treated her daughter abominably. John, for his part, resented Mrs. Powell's attempts to dominate the household.

John and Mrs. Powell were hesitant to openly express their dislike. As a result, there was a perpetual atmosphere of repressed tension in the household.

When not sleeping, reading or watching TV, John spent time with an old childhood friend, Pete Shotton. In 1965, Lennon paid £20,000 to buy Pete a half-share in a nearby supermarket. In exchange for setting him up as a grocer, Shotton more or less abandoned his family and spent his weekends hanging out with John. The two men's escapades involved a great deal of drinking and carousing.

Even at his lethargic worst, Lennon still managed to maintain his creative spark. By the fall of 1965, John's songwriting was in full blossom. Influenced by Bob Dylan, Lennon began turning out soft, acoustic based songs with poignant lyrics. One of the greatest of these numbers was "You've Got To Hide Your Love Away". This mournful ballad was allegedly directed at Brian Epstein, who kept his homosexuality far from the public eye.

John's most personal number during this period was "Norwegian Wood", a sad, dirge-like tune featuring John on acoustic guitar and George on sitar (a stringed Indian instrument). The lyrics contained coded information alluding to some of John's extramarital love affairs. If Cynthia picked up on these messages, she kept it to herself.

On 16 October 1965, the Beatles garnered international headlines after being awarded Member of the Order of the British Empire (MBE) medals. The MBE awards were given to the Beatles in recognition of their music and ability to generate profits for British industry. The band met Queen Elizabeth at a reception for MBE winners at Buckingham Palace – proof of their phenomenal embrace by mainstream society.

Not everyone was pleased at the honour bestowed upon the Beatles. A handful of British veterans of World War II returned their MBEs in protest. They felt granting the awards to a longhaired pop band cheapened their status.

True to form, Lennon reacted caustically. The veterans earned their MBEs "for killing people", John told reporters. "I'd say we deserved ours more. Wouldn't you?"

At the end of 1965, the Beatles released *Rubber Soul*, their first album to appeal to adult listeners as well as teenagers. The album contained "Norwegian Wood" and several other serious, contemplative tunes. The LP marked the beginning of a new phase in the Beatles' astonishing career.

* * *

"More popular than Jesus" is how Lennon would describe the Beatles' awesome celebrity status in early 1966. He made the remark in an interview with Maureen Cleave, the same reporter who had previously labelled him "England's laziest person".

"Christianity will go. It will vanish and shrink. I needn't argue with that. I'm right and I will be proved right. We're more popular than Jesus now", said Lennon. "Jesus was all right but his disciples were thick and ordinary. It's them twisting it that ruins it for me".

Cleave duly recorded these comments and published her article in March of that year. Few people in England took notice at the time. Had they known what twists 1966 held in store for the Beatles and their own disciples, they might have paid better attention.

The Beatles – especially John – were entering an experimental phase of their career, thanks to a little help from the psychedelic drug, LSD. Acid fired up John's imagination and inspired him to record sounds that had never been recorded before. The result of John's willingness to push the boundaries of popular music was a pair of bizarre tunes called "She Said She Said" and "Tomorrow Never Knows".

"She Said She Said" featured searing lead guitar, pounding tribal drums and a wash of sound effects. The song was a huge departure from "Love Me Do".

"Tomorrow Never Knows" was even wilder. The song contained droning sitar, bird-like sound effects, guitar feedback, drug-induced lyrics and backwards looped lead guitar. John worked closely with George Martin on this song, which marked one of the first times backwards tapes were included on a pop number.

John wasn't the only one who was busy at Abbey Road. George recorded three new songs, including a driving rocker called "Taxman". Paul's main contribution was a beautifully orchestrated tune called "Eleanor Rigby". Ringo, meanwhile, provided vocals for a delightful sing along number called "Yellow Submarine".

Before the Beatles' new album could be released, the Fab Four found themselves engulfed in a series of controversies. If the Beatles were more popular than Jesus, they were about to discover they were at least as misunderstood.

In June 1966, the band released a compilation album called *Yesterday and Today.* The cover featured the Fab Four dressed in butcher smocks cradling chunks of meat and mutilated baby dolls. The cover was supposed to be a visual pun on how the Beatles' albums were hacked up by their American distributors, who would remove tracks from the Beatles' UK releases and piece together new albums.

The cover infuriated parents and disgusted fans. Response was so negative the Beatles had to rush to create a new cover for *Yesterday and Today* featuring a less offensive shot. It was a nuisance controversy, as far as the band was concerned – but nothing like the imbroglios that were about to consume them.

A month after the *Yesterday and Today* hullabaloo, the Beatles embarked on a world tour. While the band was in Japan, Brian Epstein received an invitation for the Beatles to appear at a private party for none other than Imelda Marcos, wife of Filipino dictator, Ferdinand Marcos. Inexplicably, Epstein failed to inform the band of this imperial request.

On 4 July 1966, the Beatles performed two shows in Manila, unaware that they were supposed to be attending Ms. Marcos's private function that same day. The next morning, as the Beatles slept, the Philippine press ran hysterical stories about the band's "snub" of the first lady. Upon awakening, the Beatles realised the extent of their troubles.

The local television channel was filled with images of infuriated Filipinos. Angry crowds gathered outside the band's hotel, denouncing the Beatles. Meanwhile, inside the hotel, management cancelled room service for the band. More ominously, Philippine authorities wouldn't provide any security guards when it came time for the Beatles to leave the country.

On 6 July, the band had to make an unescorted drive to the airport, and then run the gauntlet of an angry mob to make it to their plane. The Beatles were pushed, shoved and punched as they went by. Somehow they got onboard their flight, whereupon Epstein had a breakdown and became violently sick. He was deeply upset for placing the band in such danger.

But it was in America, a few weeks later, where

controversy would reach religious proportions. In late July 1966, on the eve of their U.S. concert tour, John's comments about the Beatles being "more popular than Jesus" were reprinted in an American teen magazine called *Datebook.* In a country with a fervent evangelical Christian minority, John's remarks sparked an uproar. In some U.S. cities, former fans held bonfires of Beatles albums and memorabilia.

In the midst of this chaos, the Beatles' stunning new album was released. Called *Revolver,* it marked a giant leap for pop music.

The Beatles had no time to soak in the adoration that their latest record generated. Their entire United States tour was in jeopardy because of John's remarks about Jesus.

On 11 August 1966, Lennon faced a sea of reporters in Chicago, who demanded to know if he was going to apologise. "If I had said that television is more popular than Jesus, I might have got away with it", stated a subdued Lennon. "It's a fact, in reference to England, we meant more to kids than Jesus did, or religion at that time. I wasn't knocking it or putting it down. I was just saying it, as a fact, and it's true, more for England than here".

"I'm not saying we're better or greater or comparing us with Jesus Christ as a person or God as a thing, or whatever it is, you know, I just said what I said and it was wrong or was taken wrong and now it's all this!" Lennon continued.

While most fans accepted this *mea culpa,* hardcore critics weren't satisfied. Members of the Ku Klux Klan picketed one of the Beatles' shows. In Memphis, Tennessee, someone tossed a firework on stage as the Beatles played.

On 29 August 1966, the Beatles performed at Candlestick Park in San Francisco. That city was beginning to feel the first stirrings of the bohemian subculture known as the hippie movement. Hippies embraced music, love, drugs and long hair, and felt inclined to "drop out" of mainstream society.

The Beatles didn't stick around to check out the subculture they had partly inspired. Their performance in San Francisco was the last of the tour. All the controversy the Fab Four ran into during the 1966 tour reinforced a collective decision they had made earlier in the year. Sick of the grind, the Beatles had decided to give up touring. Their music was getting too complicated to play live and no one could hear anything anyway.

It was an astonishing decision. At the time, it was unheard of for a rock group to stop playing live. Touring was seen as essential to a band's career. After all, Elvis's refusal to perform was one of the reasons his career was in a tailspin.

The Beatles were adamant, however. No more live shows. They would become masters of the studio instead.

Chapter 5
Summer of Love

The end of touring left John Lennon with a lot of time on his hands.

Unsure of what to do next, he let himself be talked into taking part in a movie called *How I Won the War*. Richard Lester, who had worked with the Beatles on *A Hard Day's Night* and *Help!* directed the film.

The movie, set in Spain, was supposed to be a military satire. John played a shortsighted soldier named Private Gripeweed. As part of his costume, he was given a pair of round, old-fashioned wire rim glasses. For the first time, he found he didn't mind the way he looked in glasses. Increasingly, he wore them off set, and they would eventually become a kind of trademark for the rock star.

Stuck in Spain, Lennon quickly grew bored with the

cinematic process. To ease the time, he played his guitar and tried to write some new songs. One image, in particular, tumbled around in his thoughts demanding attention. Strawberry Field was the name of the neighbourhood orphanage where John loved to attend garden fetes as a boy.

As Lennon's interest in his acting work eroded, a jumble of lyrics and chords began to collect around his new song idea. He continued to work on the song – which he called "Strawberry Fields" after his return to England in the fall of 1966. But just as he had felt bored and listless in Spain, John found little of interest in his life outside of songwriting. He remained emotionally distant from Cynthia and Julian. John took massive amounts of drugs and looked for new ways to occupy his time.

On 9 November 1966, a bespectacled and befuddled Lennon found himself standing outside the Indica Gallery in London, trying to decide whether to go in. The Indica Gallery was a trendy new spot that was well known for its avant-garde shows. The place was run by John Dunbar, husband of singer/actress Marianne Faithfull, and was considered a chic place to patronise.

While the exhibit sounded interesting, Lennon's brain was muddled from all the drugs he was on. He was also very tired from having foregone sleep for a couple of days.

With nothing better to do, he stepped inside. As he made his way around, he noticed that a short, intense looking Asian woman was watching him. She had long black hair parted in the middle and was drably dressed. The dark-haired woman boldly approached John and introduced herself. Her name was Yoko Ono and she was an artist. Some of her work was on display at the Indica.

Yoko gave John a personal tour of the gallery. Lennon was amused by Yoko's exhibits. One of her "works" consisted of a board with a nail in it. Patrons were supposed to pound the nail flat with a hammer.

Another exhibit featured a ladder with a telescope at the top. The telescope was chained to a piece of canvas hanging from the ceiling. John climbed the ladder and squinted through the telescope. The telescope was focused on the word "yes" written in tiny letters on the canvas. For some reason, Lennon found this oddly reassuring. He had apparently been expecting to see a swear word.

John continued to wander around the art gallery, chatting amiably with Yoko. Then he departed, intrigued by the strange exhibits and the odd woman who had created them.

A couple of weeks after meeting Yoko Ono, John Lennon found himself fretting over a console at studio two on Abbey Road. George Martin was sitting next to him, listening intently to the song coming over the studio speakers.

John was wearing his gold-rimmed "granny glasses" and had the beginnings of a moustache. All four Beatles had recently grown facial hair, as if to signify the new course they were charting.

Lennon and Martin were listening to a demo tape of

John's new song, "Strawberry Fields Forever". The demo featured only John's voice and acoustic guitar. The lyrics to the song were idiosyncratic yet soothing, the music soft and gentle, in contrast to Lennon's typically harder-edged style. Martin thought the song was one of John's best, but Lennon wasn't sure.

When it came time to record the song with the rest of the Beatles, "Strawberry Fields" took on a strange life of its own. The end product was a world-away from the soft, acoustic number that Lennon originally envisioned.

First, the Beatles laid down multiple layers of instrumentation. Paul played a Mellotron, a keyboard instrument that sounded like a primitive Moog synthesiser. George contributed some notes on an Indian table harp, as John recorded a languid vocal track. The song that came out of these labours was slow, dreamy and drugged out.

Lennon didn't like the arrangement. Recalling the beautiful orchestral arrangement George Martin had created earlier in the year for Paul's tune, "Eleanor Rigby", John pressed the producer to write something similar.

The dutiful Martin created and recorded a score, but John still wasn't happy. He liked how the original version began and how the new version ended. John asked Martin if he could marry the two halves.

At first, Martin balked in this task; the two versions were in different keys and tempos. Splicing the songs together would sound jarring and discordant. Lennon persisted. In the midst of a phone conversation, John cheerily announced, "Don't worry, George. You can fix it", then hung up.

Martin returned to his recording console and went to work. To his surprise, he discovered that John was right. The song was fixable, with a little studio wizardry. The first version of "Strawberry Fields" was faster than the second. By speeding up the second version by roughly five percent, Martin could match the tempo of the first version. Martin spliced the two sections together and in the process, created one of the Beatles' greatest songs.

"Strawberry Fields Forever" was released as a single in February 1967. The flip side was "Penny Lane", a bright pop-ish tune by Paul that also featured lush orchestration.

In decades to come, "Strawberry Fields Forever" would be hailed as one of Lennon's best songs – if not his single greatest creation. At the time, fans weren't so sure. The tune was jarringly different than any of the Beatles' previous singles. You couldn't dance to it and the lyrics sounded like they were written on acid. The song seemed to spell the death knoll of the Beatles' cute, cuddly image.

The band was going through more than just an image change. For all his efforts on "Strawberry Fields Forever", John was rapidly ceding his leadership role in the Beatles. While happy to knock himself out on his own tunes, John no longer shaped the band's overall sound. That role had been assumed by Paul, who was becoming astonishingly prolific at the same time that John was sinking into a drug-induced stupor.

Not only had McCartney become the band's musical director, he had also taken over the day-to-day management of the Beatles, usurping Brian Epstein in the process. Brian felt left out and ignored. He suffered from depression and began taking huge quantities of amphetamines and barbiturates just to get through his day.

Like Brian, John was wary of Paul's new leadership role. He didn't dare to openly confront his old songwriting partner, however, preferring to grumble and complain.

Fortunately for their fans, John was willing to go along with Paul's ideas, including McCartney's latest brainstorm. Paul had come up with the notion of a "concept album" in which all the tunes would be thematically linked. The concept he had in mind was still a bit vague, but McCartney was certain it would blow people's minds.

Under McCartney's guidance, the Beatles worked staggeringly hard. From late 1966 to early 1967, the Fab Four spent 700 hours recording their new album. By contrast, their first record had taken less than 10 hours to record.

Producer George Martin was integral to the new shape the Beatles' music was taking. In addition to his usual role as producer, Martin arranged tunes, played instruments and crafted a mélange of sound effects.

The Beatles' new opus was entitled, *Sergeant Pepper's Lonely Hearts Club Band.* The title reflected the concept Paul finally settled on; the album was supposed to sound like a "live" recording by a group other than the Beatles. By pretending to be another act (the Lonely Hearts Club Band), the Beatles could explore new and exotic tones, textures and melodies.

While *Pepper* was Paul's idea, John did write some excellent new songs for the album. These included "Being for the Benefit of Mr. Kite" (a tribute to a Victorian-era circus act) and "Lucy in the Sky with Diamonds". "Lucy" had the same psychedelic vibe as "Strawberry Fields", and many fans spotted the initials LSD in the song's title. John insisted the real inspiration was a drawing by his son, Julian. But whether LSD in the title was coincidence or intentional, it's acid-laced atmosphere was undeniable.

The most astonishing song on the album was a Lennon and McCartney number called "A Day in the Life". The song was a hybrid – two songs joined together in one extraordinary package.

John wrote the opening, which featured mournful lyrics about death and regret backed by guitar, drums and piano. The song progressed to an orchestrated climax that was suddenly broken by Paul's chipper voice and keyboards. For the last part of the song, John took on lead vocal again. The tune worked up to a second orchestral climax then closed with a thundering piano chord.

Even the cover art for *Sergeant Pepper* was grand in scale, depicting the Fab Four wearing vivid, theatrical bandmaster uniforms. Clad in yellow, pink, blue and red outfits, with their new moustaches on full display, the Beatles looked like Field Marshals in a psychedelic army. Standing next to the Beatles was a set of waxworks figures of the band from Madame Tussaud's wax museum in London. These figures depicted the "old" Beatles, complete with pudding bowl haircuts, dark suits and ties. Behind both sets of Beatles was a wild photomontage of famous and infamous people. In front of the band an arrangement of red flowers spelled out the word "Beatles".

Sergeant Pepper's Lonely Hearts Club Band was released in June 1967. Listeners were stunned. The music and imagery on *Pepper* was far beyond that of most rock groups of the time. Critics who had previously dismissed the Beatles had to admit that *Pepper* was a pop masterpiece.

The album propelled the Beatles to a new level of superstardom. Lennon and McCartney were now rated on a par with some of the greatest composers of all time.

* * *

As John's musical partnership with Paul reached a new peak, his personal life remained chaotic. Yoko had started pursuing John – on the street and even into the studio. Yoko hung out in front of Kenwood and the studio on Abbey Road, hoping to buttonhole Lennon. During their brief encounters, she pestered him for funding and tried to interest him in new "exhibits" she was working on.

Far from being repulsed by this obsessive behaviour,

John was flattered. While plenty of groupies had lusted after him, Yoko took the hunt to new lengths. She was content to wait outside for hours in the freezing cold or pouring rain and followed her quarry everywhere. John was impressed and a little thrilled by her determination.

Short and busty, Yoko was nearly a decade older than John. Her father was a wealthy and powerful banker from Japan. Yoko had had a privileged childhood, but was a rebel from an early age. For years she had been leading an eccentric life, trying to establish herself as an avant-garde artist.

Yoko had been married twice before. The first time was in 1957, to a Japanese musician named Toshi Ichiyanagi. She soon cut her ties with Toshi and took up with Tony Cox, a charming American hustler with good connections in the artistic world.

Yoko married Tony in 1962. Unfortunately, she hadn't bothered to divorce Toshi first. Eventually, she was obliged to divorce Tony, then divorce Toshi, then remarry Tony. In 1963, Yoko had a daughter with Tony, whom she named Kyoko. Yoko surrendered the rearing of her infant to friends, family and acquaintances.

With Tony Cox at her side, Yoko set about trying to become famous. She became relatively well known in New York for her oddball artistic creations and strange performances. At one show in New York in the early 1960s, Yoko sat stoically on stage and encouraged audience members to snip off bits of her clothing with scissors.

Ever since his art school days, John had fantasised about falling in love with an assertive, bohemian woman. His current wife, Cynthia, certainly didn't fit the bill. She was neither aggressive nor particularly artistic.

For the time being, John stayed with his wife, even as Yoko pursued him. And as usual, the turmoil of his private life didn't prevent him from turning out brilliant songs.

In June 25, 1967, the Beatles played one of Lennon's compositions on a live satellite show beamed around the world. The tune was "All You Need is Love" – a paean to hippie values. The Fab Four performed the tune amidst a party-like atmosphere, with balloons and streamers festooning the room, and a crowd of celebrities – including Mick Jagger, of the Rolling Stones – joining in on the chorus.

"All You Need Is Love" was broadcast to some 400 million viewers in two-dozen countries as part of the world's first international satellite TV broadcast. The broadcast heralded the arrival of the so-called "Summer of Love". It was the advent of youth culture, spearheaded by the now blossoming hippie movement.

The new stars of this age were far removed from the rockers of the 1950s. The year 1967 saw debut albums from the likes of Jimi Hendrix, Janis Joplin and the Doors. Psychedelia was all the rage, as rock concerts began to feature wild light shows and special effects. The Beatles, too, were a very different band than the four polite, well-tailored lads who had appeared on the *Ed Sullivan Show* only three years earlier.

That summer, while embracing a new sense of spiritual awareness, the Beatles helped popularise another new trend: the growing fascination with eastern religion and altered states of consciousness. In late August, the Beatles and their spouses attended a lecture by the Maharishi Mahesh Yogi. The Maharishi was an Indian holy man who promoted Transcendental Meditation. George Harrison had met the guru in India and was deeply impressed. He convinced the others to hear the yogi speak.

The band was sufficiently intrigued to sign up for a five-day course the yogi was conducting in Bangor, Wales. On 25 August 1967, the Beatles, along with their wives and various associates, made their way to Paddington Station to take a train to Bangor.

The band's blissful retreat did not get off to a good start; after gathering at the train station, Cynthia Lennon became separated from her husband. She was held back by a police officer who thought she was just another Beatles fan. The train began pulling away, without Cynthia. John leaned out of the window and urged her to run. Freeing herself from the policeman's grasp, Cynthia tried to catch up to the departing train. She eventually gave up, and watched in tears as the train left the station for Bangor.

It was a feeling she was getting all too used to.

* * *

Initially, John was suspicious of the Maharishi. According to the guru, to achieve bliss all you had to do was meditate each day for about 30 minutes. Meditation produced a natural "high" that was healthy and invigorating, said the guru.

The Maharishi was an odd looking character, to put it mildly. He was short, with long, dirty hair and a huge beard, which gave him the appearance of a demented elf. He also had the unnerving habit of bursting into childlike giggles for no apparent reason.

For all the guru's oddball qualities, John found that he quite enjoyed the Bangor lectures. And he was relieved when Cynthia finally straggled into the retreat.

Two days after arriving at Bangor, a phone call came in from Peter Brown, who helped manage the Beatles' affairs. Brown had shocking news. Brian Epstein, the Beatles' devoted manager, was dead. Depressed since the Fab Four stopped touring, Epstein had died of an apparent drug overdose at his home.

* * *

Lennon was terrified that Brian's death meant the end of the Beatles. "The Beatles were finished when Eppy died", he recalled years later. "I knew deep inside me, that that was it. Without him, we'd had it".

Paul McCartney thought otherwise. At a band meeting held shortly after Epstein's death, Paul presented an array of plans for the future. Among other schemes, Paul wanted to shoot a new Beatles movie entitled *Magical Mystery Tour*. Ever the keen one, McCartney had written most of the script already.

John wasn't interested in making a new movie, but he didn't have any ideas of his own to propose. He reluctantly agreed to participate in the film and write some new songs for the soundtrack.

Filming for *Magical Mystery Tour* began in mid-September 1967. The Beatles insisted on making the movie themselves rather than rely on an outside director. As a result, filming was chaotic and incoherent.

The plot entailed the Beatles and an entourage of extras taking a "magical" bus trip around the English countryside. Every few minutes this trip was interrupted by an elaborate song sequence.

The best of these sequences featured John singing "I Am the Walrus". To film this part, the Beatles donned bizarre animal costumes and pranced around as John belted out the song at a piano.

The surrealism John injected into the song matched the increasingly bizarre circumstances of his home life.

In October 1967, with the *Magical Mystery Tour* film still to be released, John decided to invite his father to live with him at Kenwood. Freddie Lennon showed up at Kenwood with a young woman named Pauline Jones. This teenage university student was Freddie's new girlfriend. The two of them eagerly accepted John's offer to live with him. They stayed at Kenwood for a few weeks and then moved out to a flat rented for them by John. In addition to paying his dad's rent, Lennon put Freddie on the Beatles' payroll at £12 a week.

John's sudden embrace of his father might have had something to do with a letter penned by his Uncle Charlie. Charlie, who was Freddie's brother, felt that John deserved to hear the truth about his childhood.

Charlie outlined many of Julia Lennon's considerable flaws, including her promiscuity, the illegitimate child she gave up and her contemptible treatment of Freddie. Far from abandoning his family, Charlie pointed out, Freddie had been kicked out by Mimi and Julia. John also learned the sad tale of Freddie's failed attempt to retrieve his son in the late 1940s.

For his part, Freddie was surprised to discover that Cynthia and John were leading separate lives. Cynthia spent her evenings in London and most of her days looking after Julian. Cynthia and John largely ignored each other. Cynthia's mother, meanwhile, had left Kenwood and was now living in London.

A memorial service for Brian Epstein was held at a London synagogue in mid-October 1967. All four Beatles attended and reminisced about the man responsible for making them the most famous rock band in the world.

In November, the movie *How I Won the War* was released. It wasn't very funny and got poor reviews. Lennon's disinterest in his acting gig the previous year was all too apparent on screen.

That same month, the *Magical Mystery Tour* album was released. While the album was a smash hit – a more than worthy follow-up to *Sergeant Pepper* – the film bearing the same title bombed miserably.

The *Magical Mystery Tour* movie was not released in theatres, but broadcast on BBC television on Boxing Day. For mysterious reasons, the film was shown in black and white. All the Beatles multi-coloured imagery was reduced to tones of grey.

Critics hated the film. One newspaper referred to it as "blatant rubbish". Even hardcore Beatle fanatics had to admit that the *Magical Mystery Tour* movie was poorly made. The miserable reception that greeted the film was the first sign that the Beatles weren't infallible.

The failure of *Magical Mystery Tour* was merely the most public setback John had faced over the course of the year. The manager who had supervised every aspect of his career was dead. In Brian's stead, a giggling yogi was guiding the Beatles. Paul, meanwhile, had taken over the band's musical direction.

John's new tunes, as brilliant as they were, were soaked in a druggy haze that baffled many fans.

As 1967 came to a close, Lennon wondered how much longer he could continue on as "Beatle John".

Chapter 6
Across the Universe

The Maharishi Mahesh Yogi continued to exert a powerful pull on the Beatles. In February 1968, the band mates and their respective spouses decamped to India, where the Maharishi ran a so-called "Meditation Academy". By staying at his ashram, the Beatles hoped to gain some special spiritual insights from the guru.

Located in Rishikesh, near New Delhi, the Meditation Academy offered a peaceful, relaxing environment in which meat, alcohol and illicit drugs were forbidden. To his surprise, Lennon found that he liked being sober.

Despite the strict rules about food and intoxicants, life at the ashram was not harsh. As Ringo observed, the place was a bit like an English holiday resort camp, albeit, one that appealed to wealthy karma seekers. The luxurious grounds of Maharishi's ashram were designed with the comfort of its well-heeled patrons in mind.

The Beatles were on a relaxed regime. They were supposed to devote a few minutes each day to transcendental meditation ... maybe take in a lecture or two. Other than that, they could do as they pleased.

John, who was staying in a stone bungalow by himself, separate from Cynthia, found the arrangement ideal. After meditating, he would get out his acoustic guitar and play music for hours. At Rishikesh, he composed a series of new songs. He played his new tunes to the other Beatles, who also spent their days practising guitar and writing songs.

Just like back at home, Lennon largely ignored his wife while at the ashram. When he wasn't meditating or composing, John kept up a busy correspondence with Yoko Ono. Many of Yoko's "letters" contained nothing more than bizarre slogans or instructions, such as "HIT A WALL WITH YOUR HEAD" or "KEEP LAUGHING FOR A WEEK". John enjoyed Ono's strange missives. They appealed to his twisted sense of humour and filled him with desire for the eccentric bohemian.

But the good vibes at Rishikesh didn't last for long. Ringo and his wife, Maureen, left after only a few days. Their official excuse was that they couldn't stomach the spicy vegetarian food at the ashram. Mr. Starr apparently had a very sensitive stomach, a holdover from his sickly childhood. Soon after Ringo departed, Paul McCartney and his girlfriend, Jane

Asher, took their leave as well.

Feeling lonely now that half the Beatles were gone, John invited a friend named Alex Mardas to hang out with him at the Meditation Academy. Dubbed "Magic Alex" by his friends, Mardas portrayed himself as an electronics genius. Among other discoveries, Alex claimed to have invented a car paint that could change colour on command. It was one in a series of "inventions" that never quite worked as promised. While Alex's skills as an inventor might have been lacking, John appreciated his company.

The arrival of Magic Alex coincided with a serious crisis at Rishikesh. Some of the young female guests at the ashram began complaining that the Maharishi was sexually harassing them. Magic Alex investigated these claims and found them to be true. The Maharishi was a fake and a letch. George – who was the most spiritual of the Beatles – was particularly shocked. If the Maharishi couldn't abide by his own principles (which presumably precluded nonconsensual groping), it cast all of his teachings in doubt.

John was shaken too, largely because he considered the Maharishi as a benevolent father figure. Just as he had been disillusioned after meeting Freddie Lennon face-to-face, John was crushed to discover the Maharishi was just a dirty old man.

Lennon confronted the Maharishi and announced that the remaining Beatles and their spouses were leaving. The yogi was none too pleased. Having the world-famous Beatles at his Meditation Academy had been a public relations coup for the scruffy guru. Now his honoured guests were abruptly departing.

In a huff, the Maharishi demanded to know why Lennon was so eager to leave. "If you're so cosmic, you'll know why", Lennon snapped. Magic Alex was sent to find transportation from the ashram to the airport in New Delhi. This proved to be extremely difficult. The Maharishi had spread word that he was displeased with the Beatles. The guru had great influence in Rishikesh, both spiritual and financial. Most of the drivers Magic Alex approached were afraid the yogi would curse them if they helped the Beatles.

Finally, Magic Alex secured a pair of cars and drivers to transport Lennon and company out of the ashram. The Beatles' party managed to abscond to the New Delhi airport and away from the Maharishi.

On the plane, Lennon began knocking back drink after drink. He was angry at the Maharishi for "betraying" him. Since the yogi wasn't around, John berated his hapless wife in an angry, drunken tirade. He regaled a sobbing Cynthia with a graphic catalogue of his sexual conquests over the years. It's hard to say why John decided to come clean with his sordid, extramarital past. Perhaps he felt guilty about his own secrets and lies.

Back at Kenwood, Lennon spent several days drinking alcohol, taking drugs and complaining about the Maharishi to anyone who would listen. He also wrote a withering new song called "Maharishi" to mock the guru. John grudgingly changed the title to "Sexy Sadie" to avoid legal trouble, a decision he later regretted.

Lennon was so self absorbed, he didn't realise that the stay in Rishikesh had actually done him some good. He had been stone cold sober the entire time and had written a huge number of songs. The Maharishi might have been a fake, but life at the ashram had temporarily rejuvenated John, physically, mentally and spiritually.

John didn't see it that way. As far as he was concerned, the experience in Rishikesh had been a disaster. Even worse, he was now back in England with a wife he didn't care for and a son who annoyed him. He was eager to find an escape.

* * *

In mid-May 1968, the Beatles announced the launch of Apple Corps, a company that was supposed to serve as a cutting edge film and music firm.

Lennon recalled how Brian Epstein had struggled to get the Beatles a recording contract. John promised that Apple Corps would promote art first and profits second. He encouraged unknown artists and musicians to submit demo tapes and films to the fledgling company.

As an avalanche of submissions arrived, Apple Corps floundered in debt and financial instability. This dismal turn of events was entirely predictable; a high-end hippie clothing store called Apple Boutique – launched by the Beatles in 1967 – was also in financial dire straits. John quickly lost interest in Apple Corps, even as Paul signed up talented performers such as James Taylor.

While he had been one of the prime drivers behind the new firm, it soon became obvious that Lennon's mind was not on business.

* * *

One day in May 1968, Cynthia left Kenwood for a trip to Greece. Lennon used the occasion to invite Yoko Ono over to his house. Pete Shotton, who was now living permanently at Kenwood, greeted Yoko along with John. The trio chatted awkwardly, then Pete left the pair alone. As far as Shotton knew, Yoko was just another fan, albeit a peculiar one.

John took Yoko into a room he used as a private recording studio. He played various experimental tapes then suggested they take some acid. As the LSD kicked in, John and Yoko set about creating their own sonic experiments. The stoned pair made a series of oddball recordings that featured strange noises and Yoko's screechy voice.

After making avant-garde music, the couple undressed and made love. Both partners were still married – John to Cynthia, Yoko to Tony Cox – but it didn't seem to matter to the pair.

The next morning, Pete Shotton bumped into John on

his way to the kitchen for breakfast. John greeted Pete warmly and launched into a monologue about Yoko's wondrous qualities. Shotton was taken aback. He knew John liked Yoko, but thought that Lennon regarded her as an amusing groupie, nothing more. Now John was rambling on about ditching Cynthia and living with Yoko – with whom, John insisted, he was in love.

Shortly thereafter, Cynthia arrived. She was greeted by the sight of her husband and his new lover strutting about the house in robes. Cynthia had accepted her husband's indifference and coldness with stoic resignation, but this was too much, even for her. She packed some personal items, then marched out of her own home in shock over the end of her marriage.

* * *

In late May, the Beatles returned to the EMI studios on Abbey Road to record the huge collection of tunes they had written in India. The group had so many songs they decided to make a double album, a rarity in the late 1960s.

John's contributions included "I'm So Tired", "Happiness is a Warm Gun", "Dear Prudence" and "Sexy Sadie", among others. The double album featured a lot of loud guitar and an enormous mish-mash of styles, from hard rock to psychedelia, folk, blues, country and even ska.

While the Beatles were rocking away at Abbey Road,

Lennon began openly escorting Yoko to various functions. In the middle of June, John and Yoko planted two acorns in the grounds of Coventry Cathedral. These nuts were supposed to symbolise the union of East and West. Their fans didn't get the vague symbolism – but helped themselves to the acorns as souvenirs.

On 18 June 1968, John took Yoko to see a London play. Reporters at the event yelled at John, "Where's your wife"? Exasperated, but honest for a change, Lennon replied, "I don't know".

Actually, John and Cynthia met frequently during this period, usually with lawyers in tow, to discuss divorce.

In mid-July, while the Lennons battled in court, John, Paul and George attended the premiere of the latest Beatles movie. The film was a cartoon entitled *Yellow Submarine.* Aside from contributing a handful of new songs, the Beatles had very little to do with making the film. They didn't even provide their own voices for their cartoon avatars.

Much to their surprise, the Fab Four found they quite enjoyed *Yellow Submarine.* The movie was witty and made excellent use of the Beatles' music. The plot concerned a struggle between the upright citizens of Pepperland and a group of music-hating villains called the Blue Meanies. In the end, the Beatles saved the day by singing a series of tunes that brought the Meanies to their knees. Children and adults alike appreciated the film.

That summer, John recorded a beautiful, plaintive tune

called "Julia". The song featured some of John's most heartfelt lyrics, directed at his dead mother. It had taken him years to be able to sing openly about her.

If "Julia" was John's attempt to deal with his mother's death, "Revolution" was his first stab at a political song. The tune, an indictment of the ubiquitous self-styled revolutionaries of the late 1960s, denounced violence in a series of searing phrases.

John also recorded a number with Yoko called "Revolution Number Nine" that consisted of a weird collage of voices, sounds and disjointed snatches of music. The tune had virtually no melody, harmony or lyrics, beyond a voice repeating a number out loud, over and over.

"Revolution Number Nine" was jarring and pointless as far as Paul and George Martin were concerned, and they adamantly opposed including it on the album. John insisted. He said the song represented a new musical direction for him. In order to fit "Revolution Number Nine" on the new record, John and Paul cut one of George Harrison's compositions. George fumed, but the band's star songwriters got their way – as always.

While the Beatles continued to lay down tracks in the studio, the Apple Boutique was going bust. The enterprise was an enormous financial drain. So, on 31 July 1968, the Beatles arranged for a wild "blowout". All the stock at Apple Boutique was given away for free, with a limit of one item per customer. Afterwards, the denuded store was closed for good. Accountants estimated that the Beatles had lost over £110,000 on merchandise through their ill-considered venture into the rag trade.

By late summer, Yoko was pregnant. As a result, John gave Cynthia the go-ahead to sue him for divorce on the grounds of adultery. Cynthia was primarily concerned with retaining custody of Julian. John worried more about holding onto his money.

In late August, the Beatles released one of their greatest singles to date. The single contained the song "Hey, Jude" (written by Paul) and a speedy, hard rock version of John's "Revolution".

On 8 September 1968, the Beatles performed both songs on the David Frost TV show in Britain. The performance was filmed for later broadcast in the United States.

"Revolution" was a solid, driving tune but "Hey, Jude" stole the show. For the latter song, McCartney played keyboards and sang lead while John and George backed him on vocals and guitar. The tune featured a long, slow build-up and an equally lengthy coda, complete with a choir and orchestra.

Critics hailed "Hey, Jude" as a masterpiece. The public loved it, too. As a single, "Hey, Jude" would sell six million copies – an unheard of number at the time.

John was impressed by Paul's new tune – unaware, perhaps, of its true significance. Shortly after John and Cynthia split up, Paul had paid a surprise visit to Lennon's only son. On the way there, he began composing a song in his head for

Julian. The song was meant to cheer the little boy up.

Lennon was too preoccupied to pay much notice. In the summer of 1968, John's affair with Yoko Ono consumed him. The two of them had moved out of Kenwood and had taken up residence in a London flat owned by Ringo.

John and Yoko quickly took over the space after moving in. There, they took drugs, including heroin, and shut out the rest of the world. Their stoned revelry lasted until 18 October 1968. On that date, a squad of policemen raided the flat on the hunt for narcotics. John was hauled off and arrested for possession of an ounce of hashish. He was booked, then released on bail.

Three weeks after the raid, Yoko was rushed to hospital, where she miscarried. John moved into her hospital room during her recovery, sleeping on a mattress on the floor.

During all this tumult, John and Yoko released their first album. It was called *Unfinished Music No. 1: Two Virgins* and consisted largely of baffling sound experiments. The album was practically unlistenable, but it was the front and back covers that made it truly notorious. The front of the album featured a full frontal nudity shot of John and Yoko, standing side by side. The back featured the famous couple in the same pose, but from behind.

The release of *Two Virgins* was only one of several highlights that rounded off 1968. On 8 November, Cynthia was granted a divorce from John. Around the same time, John and Yoko moved back to Kenwood, which Cynthia and her mother had largely stripped of furniture. In the nearly empty house, John and Yoko continued their stoned, eccentric revels.

On 25 November, the Beatles' new double album was released. Its official title was *The Beatles* but everyone called it *The White Album* because the cover was completely blank. The white cover was a reaction to the ornate, gaudy covers that had graced the *Sergeant Pepper* and *Magical Mystery Tour* albums.

The White Album kicked off with Paul's bouncy rocker, "Back in the USSR" which then segued into the druggy, sluggish tones of John's "Dear Prudence". The double disc also featured "Sexy Sadie", "Julia", "Bungalow Bill" and other Lennon classics. "Revolution Number Nine" also found space on the album, although as Martin and McCartney had predicted, fans were baffled by it.

Three days after *The White Album* was released, John was fined in court for possessing cannabis. Lennon pleaded guilty to the charge, which could have brought a serious prison sentence. Instead, the judge merely fined Lennon £150. Lennon walked out of court smiling.

Chapter 7
The Ballad of John and Yoko

As 1969 began, the Beatles embarked on one of their most gruelling projects to date. McCartney thought the Beatles should get back to their roots by recording an album of simple, unadorned rock 'n' roll tunes. After laying down these new tracks in the studio, the Beatles would play them live, preferably in a spectacular locale such as a Roman amphitheatre or an ocean liner. Both the rehearsals and the live show would be filmed for posterity.

The problem was, everyone was still exhausted from the arduous recording sessions of the previous year. John didn't feel like writing new songs, while George wasn't interested in playing live. John and Yoko were taking heroin as well, which made them even more withdrawn than usual.

Through sheer force of will, Paul prevailed, and the Beatles grudgingly assembled at Twickenham Studios in early January 1969. There, the band began their filmed rehearsals.

The unforgiving movie cameras captured the Beatles in all their disarray. The band bickered like old ladies and showed little inspiration in their playing and singing. Paul provided the only flickers of energy and excitement.

McCartney had grown a beard, which made him look more mature than his band mates. His fatherly image was appropriate, as he had clearly taken charge of the Beatles.

John, meanwhile, acted like a stoned oaf, lost in his own inner world. He seemed distracted and interested only in strumming his guitar and chatting with Yoko, who sat next to him during rehearsals. Yoko's presence violated one of the Beatles' long-standing rules: no wives or girlfriends in the recording studio. Paul, George and Ringo treated John's new companion with barely disguised disgust. It was bad enough that she had invaded the Beatles' inner sanctum, but she seemed to have taken over their friend's mind, body and soul.

The Beatles continued in this dismal vein for several days. By late January, it was clear that the *Get Back* sessions, as they were now called, were a disaster.

The Beatles decided to abandon the project, but salvage something from the wreckage by playing a handful of tunes on the downtown London rooftop of Apple Corps headquarters. The location was a far cry from a Roman amphitheatre, but it would do.

Studio engineers, filmmakers, a few fans and some curious office employees joined the band as they readied their instruments. John, Paul and George stood in front of three stand-up microphones. Ringo, clad in a red waterproof jacket, sat at the ready behind his drums. A black keyboardist named Billy Preston stood to one side. Preston had been brought in to add some spark to the recording sessions.

As Yoko and a handful of other onlookers watched, the Beatles launched into their first live concert since Candlestick Park in San Francisco.

The weather was miserable, with grey, cloudy skies and a high wind. But the Beatles finally managed to find the groove that had eluded them for weeks. Their music sounded joyful and driving; like that of a young band ready to conquer the world. John and George traded guitar licks while Preston played beautiful keyboard flourishes. John and Paul handled most of the vocal duties with George offering backup.

Among other songs, Lennon sang a show-stopping rendition of a new number called "Don't Let Me Down". The tune was a tribute to Yoko.

The surprise outdoor concert drew the stunned attention of everyone in the vicinity of the Apple offices. People leaned out of windows to find out where the remarkable music was coming from. Others gazed up from the street, wondering if the band playing could possibly be the reclusive Beatles.

Not everyone appreciated the free music. Several irate shopkeepers and office managers called the police. A group of policemen marched to the top of the Apple building to cancel the impromptu concert.

The police stepped onto the roof just as Paul was singing a powerful new rock song called "Get Back". Paul threw in some improvised lyrics about playing on the rooftop as the band took the song to its climax.

The tune ended, the tiny audience applauded and the Beatles unstrapped their instruments. As the camera crews captured the moment, a smile crossed Lennon's face. He took hold of one of the microphones and made a short announcement.

"I'd like to say thanks on behalf of ourselves and the group and I hope we passed the audition", he said with a grin.

This drew laughter and another round of applause as the Beatles concluded their last live show.

* * *

In early March 1969 Lennon played another concert, this one with Yoko rather than the Beatles. The performance took place at Cambridge University and consisted of Yoko shrieking into a microphone while John extracted ear-blistering feedback from a guitar amplifier.

The oddball concert came as a relief for John, who had

been distracted by various legal and financial problems. Earlier that year, he had helped Yoko secure a divorce from Tony Cox. Yoko got her divorce, but it cost John dearly. As part of the divorce agreement, Lennon agreed to pay off various joint debts incurred by Tony and Yoko. These debts came to roughly £100,000. John spent more money on Yoko's divorce than his own.

Making John's financial situation even more precarious, the Beatles had become entangled in a ferocious battle over money. John, George and Ringo wanted to hire Allen Klein, a high-profile accountant turned manager, to go over their financial situation. Klein was a notorious figure who had briefly managed the Rolling Stones and was known as a brilliant numbers man. Klein promised he could untangle the Beatles' very confusing business affairs and get them more money.

Paul had other ideas. He was marrying a young American woman named Linda Eastman, whose brother, John, happened to be a top-notch lawyer. Paul wanted to hire John Eastman to handle the Beatles' finances.

Paul's band mates weren't keen on having Paul's in-laws exert so much control over their fiscal affairs. They feared any deal with John Eastman would favour Paul over the rest of them. Eventually, the Beatles voted three to one to appoint Klein as their business advisor.

Klein went through the Beatles' papers and quickly discovered that Epstein's mismanagement had lost the band millions of pounds. Under Epstein, the Beatles had been subject to a very low royalty rate on their albums. They had been paid just over £5,000 each for their first movie, at a time when they could have commanded 10 times that figure.

As Klein sorted out the Beatles' finances, John and Yoko continued their symbiotic journey. A couple of weeks after their "concert" at Cambridge University, they flew to Gibraltar to get married. Yoko wore a white mini dress for the occasion. John wore a white jacket with white training shoes, and smoked throughout the ceremony, which was held in the British Consulate.

On 22 March 1969, John and Yoko began their honeymoon at the Amsterdam Hilton in the Netherlands. There, they staged the first of their infamous "bed-ins". This involved spending a week in bed, doing interviews with the press and promoting world peace – John's latest *cause du jour*.

"Just suppose we had wanted to go to Capri for a secret honeymoon, like Jackie Kennedy had", Lennon told an interviewer in later years. "The press would have been bound to find out. So we thought we might as well do something constructive with the publicity".

"Our life is our art", John added. "That's what the bed-ins were. When we got married, we knew our honeymoon was going to be public anyway, so we decided to make a statement. We sat in bed and talked to reporters for seven days. It was hilarious".

The bed-ins didn't feature much sleeping, at least during the day. The Lennons did interviews from 10 a.m. to 10 p.m., with different teams of photographers and reporters. War, according to John and Yoko, was bad. Violence was evil and peace was good. These opinions were common in the late 1960s when opposition to the U.S.-led war in Vietnam was widespread. Such sentiments had never been expressed in such a unique fashion, however.

At the conclusion of their Amsterdam bed-in, John and Yoko decamped to Vienna. There, they talked to the press from inside a giant bag. John told the assembled reporters that "bagism" was about "total communication, without prejudice". Yoko, for her part, sang a Japanese folk song to the bewildered media.

More madness would follow. That spring, John mailed dozens of acorns to world leaders. This project was called "Nuts for Peace". In the view of Beatles fans around the globe, who regarded John and Yoko's adventures with a sense of stunned disbelief, the name was entirely appropriate.

* * *

May 1969 was a big month for John Lennon. On the fifth, he purchased a beautiful Georgian-era mansion called Tittenhurst Park in rural Berkshire. The mansion included 72 acres of land. Lennon had the place elaborately fitted for sound, and installed a professional 16-track recording studio. Film projection and editing rooms were also added, as the Lennons planned on unleashing a series of experimental movies.

At George Harrison's suggestion, Lennon hired a group of local Hare Krishnas to assist with reconstruction work at his new home. With their shaved heads, celibate lifestyles and affinity for chanting and dancing, the Hare Krishnas were one of the more colourful cults to emerge in the late 1960s. Unfortunately for John, they were terrible workers. He eventually kicked them off his property and hired professional labourers.

Also in May, the Beatles signed a three-year management contract with Allen Klein. Paul voted against bringing Klein on board, but went along with the majority decision. Klein's big mission was to renegotiate the Beatles' contracts with their record company, EMI. If Klein was successful, John, Paul, George and Ringo stood to gain a fortune.

Lennon was also busy in the studio. That spring, he wrote and recorded a bouncy tune called "The Ballad of John and Yoko". Paul contributed piano and drums to the number, which was otherwise a solo effort from John. The song chronicled the Lennons' recent activities and attacked critics who were out to "crucify" John. The lyrics were self-pitying, but the tune was boppy and the song was another chart-topper for the Beatles.

In late May, John and Yoko decided to hold a 10-day bed-in for peace in Montreal, Canada. The famous pair set up shop in the swanky Queen Elizabeth Hotel where they held forth to hordes of reporters.

The Montreal bed-in was mostly notable for the

unorthodox recording method of one of Lennon's greatest songs. The song, "Give Peace a Chance", was recorded in the Lennons' hotel suite with a choir made up of fans and celebrities. Among those who chimed in on the song's famous refrain were comedian Tommy Smothers, a clutch of Hare Krishnas and LSD guru Timothy Leary.

"Give Peace a Chance" became an anthem of the anti-Vietnam War movement. As wacky as Lennon had become, his music and words still had the power to inspire and motivate.

* * *

In June 1969, John went on one of the more ill-fated road trips of his life. That month, he convinced Yoko to journey to Scotland with him to visit Lennon family relatives. John had fond memories of the Scottish highlands from childhood, and wanted to share his Celtic experiences with his new wife.

For some reason, Yoko ordered John to drive the entire way from southern Britain to the highlands. Perhaps she felt this would make the Lennons seem more like an ordinary family. John, however, was not an ordinary family man. He barely knew how to drive, and he had terrible vision. Despite his profound misgivings, John caved in. He found it difficult to say no to his new wife.

Grudgingly, he loaded up his Mini. Then, with Yoko, her daughter Kyoko (who was visiting Britain with Tony Cox) and his son Julian, John began the long journey to Scotland.

Lennon didn't know how to change gears properly, however, and quickly wrecked the Mini's gearbox.

John ditched the Mini and arranged for his chauffeur to drive up with a second vehicle, a white Maxi. It would have made sense for the chauffeur to transport the Lennons on the final leg of their journey, but Yoko wouldn't hear of it. Once more, John had to take the wheel.

Somehow, John made it to northern Scotland, where he had a joyous reunion with his relatives. Yoko, however, behaved childishly and barely spoke to John's Scottish family.

One day, John decided to drive his family to visit a glacial bay. The trip was not a success. While driving on a narrow road, Lennon panicked at the sight of an oncoming car. He drove the Maxi into a ditch, injuring Yoko and Kyoko in the process. Yoko required 14 stitches on her face.

The accident infuriated John's former wife, Cynthia. She stormed up to Scotland and retrieved her son, without speaking to either John or Yoko.

* * *

By summer 1969, it was clear that the album and movie that were supposed to have come out of the January "Get Back" recording sessions would not be forthcoming. The Beatles felt their songs and recordings weren't up to scratch. A great deal of post-production work would be required to make the tracks releasable. No one had the stomach to oversee such a production.

In order to have a record out that year, the Beatles were forced to return to EMI studios in early July. As John would relate later, all four Beatles seemed to know that the summer sessions would be the Beatles' last. As a result, the band was temporarily willing to put aside personal animosities for the sake of recording their swan song.

Even the presence of Yoko couldn't spoil the atmosphere. Still in recovery from the car accident in Scotland, Yoko took up residence in the studio in a hospital bed. Lying on her back, she would knit and read and watch her husband. The other Beatles shook their heads in disbelief but said nothing.

Once again, Paul dominated the sessions. Under McCartney's direction, the Beatles recorded a suite of short compositions with titles such as "Mean Mister Mustard" and "Polythene Pam". The suite represented some of the most superb material the Beatles had ever done.

The sessions were also notable for the inclusion of two of George's best songs, "Here Comes the Sun" and "Something". The latter tune would become a number one hit single.

John's contributions leaned towards basic rock. His new numbers included "Come Together" and "She's So Heavy", both of which featured searing vocals and loud guitar.

On 22 August 1969, the Beatles gathered in a park for a photo session. By this point, Lennon had grown a bushy beard. With the black hat he wore for the photo session and his shoulder length hair, he looked like a rabbi.

The photo session wasn't particularly remarkable. It was, however, the last one the Beatles ever participated in as a full group. By the time the pictures were published, the Beatles had fallen apart.

Chapter 8
The Plastic Ono Band

John was relieved when the Beatles' latest recording session finally came to a close. As always, however, he was daunted by the prospect of having to find something else to do.

John might have slipped back into his normal, post-album lethargy, but for a timely phone call in early September 1969. The call came from John Brower, a Canadian promoter who was organising a rock 'n' roll revival show in Toronto. Various greats from the 1950s, including Chuck Berry, Fats Domino and Bo Diddley, had been booked to perform. Brower asked Lennon if he felt like attending as a guest of honour.

The thought of being at a concert with so many of his childhood heroes intrigued John. He told the promoter he might be interested in showing up, but only on one condition – that he be allowed to perform. Astonished, Brower jumped at the chance to have a Beatle headline his concert. He agreed to give a spot to John.

Lennon could have asked the Beatles if they wanted to perform. Instead, he decided that the show in Toronto would mark his debut as a solo artist. He threw a makeshift band together, consisting of Eric Clapton on lead guitar, Alan White on drums and Klaus Voormann, an old friend from the Beatles' Hamburg days, on bass.

This ragtag outfit rushed to the airport where they boarded the last possible plane for Toronto. Lennon led a half-hearted rehearsal on the airplane with unamplified instruments, but other than that, his band was totally unprepared.

Nevertheless, Lennon was cavalier. The group would largely play 1950's rock 'n' roll standards that everyone knew. With a bit of luck and the support of the talented musicians around him, John was confident he could make it through his first full solo concert.

Once they reached Toronto, the band stumbled out of the plane and into a waiting limo. The limo – driven by one of Brower's staff – rushed to Varsity Stadium with a protective phalanx of bikers alongside who acted as a scruffy security detail. On arrival at the stadium, they were greeted by thunderous applause. The ecstatic greeting only served to unnerve John, whose confidence was beginning to unravel. He had very bad preshow jitters, a condition made worse by the fact that both he and Eric Clapton were suffering from heroin withdrawal. As wild as they were, the rockers hadn't dared to bring any drugs with them on the plane, for fear of getting nabbed at customs.

Brower managed to secure some cocaine for the sickly rock stars. Once he got high, John no longer felt so nervous.

After what seemed like an endless wait, John finally got his cue. Guitar in hand, he walked stiffly onto the stage, followed by his band. The fans went berserk again, as John's group assumed their places on stage. Wearing a blindingly bright white suit, John faced the adoring crowd. He admitted the band had never played before, then kicked off a ragged but furious set. To John's delight, the sound system on stage was so powerful it drowned out the cries of the audience. Music technology had advanced enormously since the Beatles quit touring.

The group blasted their way through "Dizzy Miss Lizzie", "Money" and "Blue Suede Shoes". They even tackled a few Lennon originals, including "Yer Blues" from *The White Album*, "Give Peace a Chance" and the yet to be released "Cold Turkey".

The band was loose and sloppy, each musician desperately trying to stay in time and play the right notes. John's voice sounded screechy and raw. But the crowd loved every minute of Lennon's appearance.

John led the group through a clutch of tunes, then Yoko took centre stage, microphone in hand. Yoko thrust the microphone to her face then began emitting a series of shrieks and wails. The superstar band stopped playing music and concentrated on getting feedback from their amplifiers. Yoko's "song" was entitled, "Don't Worry Kyoko (Mommy's Only Looking for her Hand in the Snow)".

The crowd was not impressed. Their cheers turned to boos. Before long, audience members were hurling dirt and debris at Yoko, furious that this screeching diva would dare to occupy the same stage as her husband.

The Toronto concert was clearly a mixed success, but John was delighted nonetheless.

* * *

John returned to London in good spirits, ready to face his fellow band-mates at a board meeting called by Paul.

The meeting was held one week after the rock 'n' roll show in Toronto. The purpose of the gathering was to determine the Beatles' next career move. As usual, Paul led the discussion. To no one's surprise, he suggested that they record another album and go on tour.

Lennon shot down all of Paul's proposals. Abruptly, he made an announcement he had been stewing over for some time. John was leaving the band. He said he wanted to "divorce" the Beatles, just as he had divorced Cynthia.

His decision shocked everyone in the room. Paul in particular was stunned. He knew John was disgruntled, but never imagined Lennon was willing to break up the band. No one spoke as John got to his feet and bolted from the meeting. He was eager to go public with the news of his departure. Allen Klein – who was now managing most of the Beatles' business affairs – convinced him otherwise.

Earlier that month, Klein scored a huge victory for the band. He had successfully renegotiated their record contracts with EMI for the North American market, where sales were highest. The Beatles' first contract, as negotiated by Brian Epstein, provided the band with a mere six cents per album in royalties. By 1967, they earned 40 cents an album, a sizeable increase, but still a low rate by rock-star standards.

Under Klein's deal, which came into effect in mid-1969, the Beatles' North American royalties jumped to 57 cents an album. This figure was scheduled to rise to 72 cents in the early 1970s.

Klein didn't want to jeopardise this new royalty arrangement through any rash actions on the part of the Fab Four. Lennon reluctantly agreed to keep silent for the time being. There would be no official talk about a Beatles breakup, even as the band mates went their separate ways.

Ironically, the Beatles fell apart just as they were hitting a new artistic peak.

The tunes they had recorded in the summer were compiled on an album called *Abbey Road*, which was released to enormous fanfare in the autumn of 1969. Critics fell all over themselves praising the record. Some hailed it as the best work the Beatles had ever done.

Meanwhile, a whole new album, containing material from the aborted "Get Back" sessions, was waiting in the wings. So was all the film that had been shot of the band at Twickenham and on the roof of the Apple offices.

Lennon forged ahead as a solo artist, even as the accolades continued to pile up for the Beatles latest work. In late October, he released a single called "Cold Turkey" that featured whiplash guitar and impassioned lyrics about heroin addiction. John credited its composition to "John Lennon and the Plastic Ono Band" rather than the Beatles.

He also continued to press forward with his oddball peace projects. In late November, he returned his Member of the Order of the British Empire award to the Queen. He included a note reading, "Your majesty, I am returning your MBE in protest against Britain's involvement in the Nigeria-Biafra thing, against our support of the American troops in Vietnam and against 'Cold Turkey' slipping down the charts. With love, John Lennon".

Two weeks later, Lennon released a solo album called *Live Peace in Toronto* which contained the songs he played at the rock 'n' roll revival show. It sold quite well, despite the inclusion of Yoko's vocal contributions.

Shortly before Christmas, John and Yoko put up huge billboards in a dozen cities around the world containing the words, "War Is Over! If You Want it, Happy Xmas from John and Yoko".

The billboard campaign was the opening shot of what

John intended to be an all-out war on war.

A week before Christmas, John and Yoko flew to Canada to announce plans for a huge peace concert to be held in Ontario in 1970. John said this concert would outdo the Woodstock Festival (which saw hundreds of thousands of young people gather peacefully for an outdoor show in upstate New York). He promised an exceptional lineup for his festival, which was now being called "The Music and Peace Conference of the World". Lennon told reporters he wanted Elvis Presley to headline the event. John hoped to sing a duet with The King, which would be broadcast on satellite TV around the world. Lennon hired John Brower, the same man who put on the Toronto rock 'n' roll revival concert, to organise and promote the event.

The Lennons set up a temporary headquarters at the Toronto-area farm of singer Ronnie Hawkins, an Arkansas boy who worked the Canadian rock 'n' roll revival circuit. They spent a few days at this bucolic locale, communicating with bands and promoters about the forthcoming peace festival. The Lennons spent hours working the phones – so much so that Ronnie later received a phone bill for $5,000.

During their Canadian sojourn, John and Yoko also met Canadian Prime Minister Pierre Trudeau in Ottawa. Their chat centred on the peace festival, drugs, rock 'n' roll, war and the youth movement. Trudeau was the first politician who impressed John. After the meeting, Lennon told reporters, "If there were more leaders like Mr. Trudeau, the world would have peace".

As it turned out, peace was in short supply that winter, despite John's best intentions.

* * *

If anything is clear from John Lennon's career, it is that any new and bold undertaking requires an equally new, equally bold hairdo. Perhaps Lennon knew it by instinct. As he contemplated his latest plans for peace and enlightenment, his appearance underwent a transformation.

This transformation took place in Jutland, a remote part of Denmark. Yoko's ex-husband, Tony Cox, was living there with his new partner, Melinde Kendall. Tony and Melinde both taught at an experimental school. The Lennons dropped by shortly after Christmas to visit Yoko and Tony's daughter, Kyoko, and to discuss the little girl's custodial arrangements.

After arriving in Jutland, Cox insisted that all the adults present consume a special concoction of hashish paste. Once everyone was thoroughly stoned, Melinde and Cox held forth on UFOs and other strange topics. According to Cox, the pair was in regular communication with beings from another planet.

Normally, John might have scoffed at such claims. High as he was, communications with extraterrestrials seemed not just possible, but advisable. And then, in a leap of logic that only the extravagantly stoned could hope to understand,

John was seized with insight: he had to cut off all his hair.

He did just that – and Yoko and Kyoko followed suit.

The stoned, skin-headed Lennons departed from Jutland intent on a new mission. The Music and Peace Conference of the World would now have an out-of-this-world angle to it. John told John Brower that the festival had to be completely free. He insisted that some of Cox's fellow UFO enthusiasts be included in the plenary sessions for the festival.

John also dreamed up an oddball electoral campaign. His notion was to flood each country in the world with "peace ballots". These ballots would ask citizens if they were for or against peace. Once voting was completed, the results would be tabulated, then an International Peace Party would be set up in every nation where peace had won a majority.

If talk about a global election didn't unnerve the promoters of the Music and Peace Conference of the World, Tony Cox's UFO-espousing friends certainly did. Cox's buddies announced that John and Yoko would make their appearance at the festival on board a levitating car powered by psychic energy.

John Brower and the other promoters were exasperated. By mid-February, the situation had come to a head. Brower insisted he couldn't possibly stage the show for free – a minimum of one dollar per person would be required to recoup festival costs.

Lennon's head, however, was still in the cosmic clouds. He pulled out of the festival then penned an incoherent screed for *Rolling Stone* magazine. Published in the spring of 1970, John's essay offered a one-sided take on the failure of the Toronto peace festival.

"We still hoped that the larger concept of the peace festival and its karmic effects on the world had lifted [John Brower] out of the bread hang-up scene and he would turn on to being a peace promoter", wrote John. Lennon capped his rant with the query, "Have we forgotten what vibes are"?

Lennon himself was clearly picking up vibes from a very strange and distant place – but they didn't hurt his music in any way. On 26 January 1970, in a day-long blast of inspiration, John wrote, recorded and mixed a new tune called "Instant Karma". To assist him on the recording, John recruited George Harrison, Klaus Voormann and Alan White.

John decided not to use George Martin as producer. Instead, he called in Phil Spector, a brilliant, if unstable, American studio genius. Spector was short and very eccentric. He was notoriously possessive of his girlfriends and completely paranoid about perceived threats to his well being.

Eccentricities aside, Spector was very talented. He had recorded some of the biggest "girl band" hits of the mid-1960s. Spector was renowned for pioneering the "wall of sound" effect by recording multiple layers of instrumentation and vocals.

Spector did an excellent job with "Instant Karma". The song contained rolling, tribal drums, crystal clear vocals and pounding keyboards. The tune was unsettling but catchy.

They released "Instant Karma" as a single only weeks after recording it.

John was so delighted he invited Spector to salvage what he could from the *Get Back* tapes. It's unclear whether John bothered to check with the other Beatles before handing over the recordings. Paul would later accuse his former songwriting partner of working behind his back.

Spector had always wanted to produce the Beatles. He eagerly went to work, ploughing through hundreds of hours of tape in search of a few good songs.

As Spector laboured on the *Get Back* sessions, John took stock of his life in recent months – his departure from the Beatles, the Peace Conference fiasco and his own detachment from reality.

In an effort to regain his sanity and clear his drug-befuddled head, John, along with Yoko, visited a private London drug clinic in March. The clinic catered to a wealthy clientele and knew how to be discrete about the various afflictions and addictions of their customers.

John and Yoko left the clinic with a supply of methadone, a synthetic opiate used to ease symptoms associated with heroin withdrawal. They were eager to stop using hard drugs once and for all, and get on with their lives as an ex-Beatle and his wife.

Chapter 9

New York, New York

Back on the straight and narrow, John Lennon's new kick came in the form of a book, not a drug. The book was *The Primal Scream,* written by a California psychologist named Arthur Janov. The book arrived in John's mail in early 1970 – part of a publicity effort on Janov's part to garner celebrity endorsements for his work.

According to Janov, adults could achieve mental serenity by reliving the turbulent emotions they had felt as children. "Primal scream therapy" as Janov called it, involved a lot of screaming, yelling and crying. Indulging in such feelings was supposed to provide a cathartic release.

John was transfixed. As someone with serious emotional scars from childhood, he was intrigued by Janov's ideas.

John also liked the idea of screaming your way to health, as it closely corresponded to his primal singing style.

John arranged for the offbeat psychologist to journey to Britain to conduct personal one-on-one sessions with both of the Lennons. A charismatic healer, Janov convinced John and Yoko to travel to California for a more intensive therapeutic regime.

So, in late April 1970, John and Yoko flew to Los Angeles, where they enrolled in Janov's primal scream therapy group. Three times a week, the Lennons showed up to rage, bellow and holler on cue.

John had plenty to be angry about. For one thing, Paul had broken the gentleman's agreement not to reveal the breakup of the Beatles. In a solo album released that spring, McCartney included a notice stating that he had left the band. Having concluded that they would never get back together, Paul wanted to tell the world about the Beatles' breakup. John was furious. He had been the first one to leave the band but had kept silent.

Ironically, the Beatles still had plenty of material to release, even if they were no longer recording together. In May, a film and album containing the songs recorded for the *Get Back* project were finally released. Retitled *Let It Be*, the film captured some of the tensions that had torn the Beatles apart. Fans were horrified to see their heroes bicker and argue with each other on screen. Even the electrifying footage of the Beatles playing on the roof of the Apple headquarters couldn't sweeten the sour tone of the film.

The *Let It Be* album sounded nothing like what the Beatles had intended. While the original plan had been to record a stripped down rock 'n' roll record, producer Phil Spector had added a thick layer of studio gloss to many of the songs. Two songs, Paul's "The Long and Winding Road" and John's "Across the Universe" were particularly marred by the presence of violins, harps and angelic choir voices.

McCartney hated Spector's treatment but John didn't seem to mind. In fact, he hired Spector to oversee his first solo album in the summer of 1970. John used very few outside musicians for his debut. Ringo played drums, Klaus Voormann handled bass, while Billy Preston contributed some keyboards. John played all the other instruments – primarily guitar – himself.

Having laid his soul bare in primal scream therapy, John decided to keep his record painfully raw and honest. To this end, he recorded a clutch of harsh, yet powerful tunes such as "Mother" (about Julia Lennon), "Working Class Hero" and "God".

Before his solo album could be released, Lennon invited his father to Tittenhurst Park for a confrontational visit. Freddie Lennon arrived in October, with his young wife, Pauline, and their toddler in tow.

Before Freddie even sat down, John pounced. He unleashed a primal scream on his father, raving at him for abandoning him as a boy. John blasted his mother, Julia as "a whore" who ruined his life.

Freddie Lennon, who thought he had been invited for a pleasant social visit, was stunned by this ferocious verbal assault. Whenever he tried to calm John down or interrupt his monologue, Lennon became even angrier.

Primal scream therapy had convinced John of the benefit of releasing bottled-up emotions. To this end, he screeched and wailed and ranted at his father about his terrible childhood in Liverpool.

At one point, Freddie's young son became alarmed and tried to hide. John pointed at the boy and screamed, "See what will happen to him if you lock him away from his parents and shut him up with a mad woman! He'll end up a raving lunatic, like me!"

In the course of his rant, Lennon told Freddie to get out of his life. Freddie needed no prodding. He raced out of Tittenhurst Park with Pauline and their child, never to return.

* * *

Two momentous events occurred in December 1970. On 11 December, John's solo album was released. Entitled, *John Lennon/Plastic Ono Band,* the album was widely praised by critics. Fans, however, were largely turned off by its abrasiveness. The instrumentation on the tracks was primitive and raw, the lyrics angry and bitter. The sparse songs sounded nothing like the lush tones and beautiful harmonies of the Beatles.

John wasn't concerned by what the fans thought. He had recorded the album to exorcise his demons and establish himself as a serious solo artist, not to sell millions of copies.

A similar motivation guided John in his epochal interviews with *Rolling Stone* magazine. Jann Wenner, the publisher of *Rolling Stone*, recorded a series of interviews with John over several days in December. The interviews captured Lennon at his most acerbic and angry.

Lennon described the Beatles as "the biggest bastards on earth" whose tours consisted of nonstop debauchery. He dismissed the entire late 1960's counter-culture and protest movement as ineffectual and insipid.

"The people who are in control and in power and the class system and the whole bullshit bourgeois scene is exactly the same, except that there's a lot of ... middle class kids with long hair walking around London in trendy clothes", Lennon told Wenner. "The dream is over, it's just the same, only I'm thirty and a lot of people have got long hair, that's all".

To cap the interviews, Lennon announced that he "resented performing for fuckin' idiots who won't know – and don't know – anything".

The interviews were published over two issues of *Rolling Stone* magazine in January and February 1971. Beatles fans were horrified. It was as if someone had lifted the mask off the Beatles to reveal a leering monster underneath.

* * *

In mid-1971, Lennon began work on his second solo album. Unlike his debut, his new record would be a polished affair, with a pop slant and none of the bile of its predecessor.

The most famous song on the album was the title track, "Imagine". A simple piano tune, the track invited listeners to imagine peace. In time, it would become a Lennon classic.

As John worked on his album, Yoko launched a campaign to get her husband to relocate from Britain to New York City. NYC was Yoko's adopted home town and the place where she felt she belonged. Lennon was uncomfortable with the idea of moving. He feared he might be overwhelmed in New York.

With Yoko's prodding, the Lennons began making lengthy visits to New York. As he was a British citizen, Lennon acquired a six-month nonrenewable visa to stay in the United States.

In August 1971, John and Yoko took up residence at the swanky St. Regis Hotel in Manhattan. They set about hiring a large staff to promote their art. Among their hires was a young, hard-working Asian girl named May Pang. Pang soon became an indispensable part of the Lennon entourage.

In addition to music and painting, John and Yoko decided to make movies. Their films were highly experimental, if not totally off-putting. One short, entitled *Fly*, featured close-ups of a fly bouncing on a nude woman's body. *Two Virgins* consisted of inter-cut shots of John and Yoko's faces while *Self Portrait* featured a close-up of Lennon's penis.

During this period, Yoko recorded a solo album of her own, which was also called *Fly*. John performed on the record and promoted it to reporters. The public hated it, however, and Yoko's album was a washout. *Imagine* enjoyed considerably more success. It was released in September and sold very well. Critics praised it and eagerly looked forward to more Lennon solo material.

John, however, was more interested in leading a revolution than in making music. In the autumn of 1971, he suddenly embraced the radical "counter-culture" that he had previously scorned.

Throughout his career, John had been in sync with the cultural zeitgeist. For once his timing was off; by late 1971, it was obvious that the hippie youth/protest movement was on life-support. Peace and love didn't pay the rent and most hippies had gone back to study or work. The U.S., meanwhile, was withdrawing troops from Vietnam, a move that triggered a precipitous decline in anti-war activism.

Lennon seemed oblivious. Having flirted with LSD, Transcendental Meditation, world peace and primal scream therapy, radical politics became his latest pet cause. He began hanging out with self-styled activists such as Jerry Rubin and Abbie Hoffman, who had been instrumental in organising anti-Vietnam war protests in the late 1960s.

On 10 December 1971, Lennon played a benefit concert for John Sinclair, the manager for the "political" hard-rock group MC5. An outspoken radical, Sinclair had been given a harsh jail sentence for a minor marijuana violation.

The Sinclair benefit was held in Ann Arbor, Michigan, one of the last enclaves of the hippie movement. At 3 a.m., following a long lineup of performers, John and Yoko appeared on stage toting acoustic guitars.

"We came here tonight to say that apathy isn't it. And that we can all do something", John told the crowd. "So Flower Power didn't work. So what! We can start again".

On that note, Lennon sang a handful of new tunes, with titles such as "Attica State" and "John Sinclair".

A few days later, John and Yoko performed at a benefit concert for victims of a prison uprising at Attica State Penitentiary. After that, they attended a street demonstration in favour of the Irish Republican Army (IRA) terrorist organisation.

Considering that Lennon, a British citizen, was staying in the U.S. on a temporary visa, his flirtation with the radical-left was not the most expedient thing politically. Indeed, the federal U.S. government kept close tabs on him. The government was concerned that John might encourage young people to vote against president Richard Nixon in the upcoming elections.

In January 1972, Strom Thurmond, a conservative Senator from South Carolina and member of the Judiciary

Subcommittee of the Senate Internal Security Committee, wrote a memo to his superiors. The Senator noted how Lennon was hanging out with known radicals and suggested the U.S. government terminate his visa.

A few weeks later, John's visa expired. He received a renewal, but it only lasted for a few days. On 6 March 1972, the New York Immigration and Naturalization Service cancelled Lennon's visa extension, at the urging of Attorney General John Mitchell's office. The government denied John's visa ostensibly because of his 1968 drug conviction. Whatever the real reason, it looked very much like John was about to be deported back to Britain.

In a display of defiance, Lennon entered a New York studio in March to record a series of strident protest numbers. He used Phil Spector as his producer and a group called Elephant's Memory as his backup band.

The album that came out of these sessions was called *Some Time in New York City*. The songs on the record covered an array of causes, including racism, feminism, peace, radical politics and drug laws. The music was mediocre, the lyrics polemical and harsh. Unsurprisingly, the record bombed. It sold a meagre 300,000 copies – far less than either of John's first two solo albums.

John wanted to go on tour in the summer of 1972, right before the U.S. presidential election. He hoped to use the tour to hype his career and promote a variety of far-left causes. In particular, he wanted to use his time on stage to criticise the

Nixon administration for continuing the war in Vietnam.

Beyond two concerts at New York City's Madison Square Garden in August 1972, the tour never got off the ground. The shows featured John and Yoko backed by Elephant's Memory. John ran through a series of solo numbers, including "Mother" and "Cold Turkey" and played the Beatles song, "Come Together". Yoko stood by his side, swaying expressionlessly and occasionally braying into a microphone.

John became too tangled in legal matters to play any more concerts that year. Instead of going on tour, he hired an immigration lawyer named Leon Wildes to fight for his right to stay in America. In the meantime, he pinned his hopes on Richard Nixon's defeat.

On 7 November 1972, John and Yoko attended a party at Jerry Rubin's apartment in New York City to watch the U.S. presidential election results. To the dismay of everyone present, President Richard Nixon cruised easily to a reelection victory. John feared that Nixon's reelection would lead to his deportation. Lennon began to drink heavily. He started screaming and ranting. Guests tried to calm him down, which only aggravated him more.

As far as John was concerned, his "radical" activities of the past two years had achieved absolutely nothing. His attempt to overthrow the Nixon administration through the power of music had been a dismal failure.

It was time to move on.

* * *

In the months after the 1972 presidential election, Lennon wallowed in self-pity. Convinced he was going to be deported at any moment, he did little but drink and take drugs.

Yoko was annoyed. She wanted to get her own solo career going, and was tired of dealing with her husband's antics. To distract John, Yoko convinced May Pang to become John's mistress. Yoko wanted May to provide John with sexual and emotional support while she concentrated on becoming a pop star.

John didn't object to the arrangement. After Yoko explained her plans to him, he latched onto May and pursued a torrid affair. May was deeply ambivalent about her new role, but remained obedient to Yoko's strange dictums.

When John and May moved to Los Angeles in 1973, Yoko was entirely supportive. She relied on May to keep her husband in line. If asked by reporters, John and May were supposed to deny they were having an affair.

The party line was that John had moved out to the West Coast to record an album of rock 'n' roll standards with producer Phil Spector. Why John had to do this in Los Angeles wasn't clear.

When he wasn't recording rock 'n' roll classics, Lennon spent his time in nightclubs and at parties. He divided his time between Los Angeles and New York, usually with May Pang at his side.

By abandoning politics for partying, John caught up with the times once again. A new era, dubbed the "me decade" had emerged from the wreckage of the idealistic '60s. Changing society was no longer seen as a worthy goal. Self-indulgence was the ethos of the day. As a fixture on the nightclub scene, Lennon epitomized the hedonistic spirit of the times.

In the fall of 1974, he wrote an excellent song called "Whatever Gets You Thru the Night". Rock star Elton John participated in the recording session, and extracted an unlikely promise from the reclusive Lennon. Elton asked John to perform live with him if the song topped the charts. Convinced that his single would never be a hit, Lennon agreed.

As it turned out, "Whatever Gets You Thru the Night" reached number one, and John had to make good on his promise. On 28 November 1974, Lennon joined Elton John on stage at Madison Square Garden to perform the song. Lennon also played "Lucy in the Sky With Diamonds" and another even older Beatles tune.

"I thought we'd do a number by an old estranged fiancé of mine called Paul", said John, by way of announcing a performance of "I Saw Her Standing There".

Yoko Ono secretly attended the concert, and watched her husband perform. When the show was over, John and Yoko had a poignant backstage reunion. John wanted to come home. As much as he liked May, he longed for the security Yoko provided. Yoko, however, wasn't interested in having John back. She thought he was still too unbalanced. Also, Yoko wanted to keep plugging her own musical career, such as it was.

The thousands of fans at Madison Square Garden had no inkling of this backstage drama. They continued to whoop and cheer, long after the house lights went on, delighted by the surprise appearance of a former Beatle. As it turned out, it was the last concert John ever performed.

* * *

By early 1975, John was ready for yet another drastic life-change. Yoko, afraid that John was getting too attached to May, finally agreed to have him back. She worried that if she didn't, John might ditch her and marry May – just as he had ditched Cynthia.

John, on the other hand, seemed delighted to be allowed back home by Yoko. He dropped the heartbroken May and moved into the Dakota (the posh New York apartment where Yoko was now living) in March 1975.

This reunion made headlines around the world. When asked by *Newsweek* magazine about his decision to return to Yoko, John was ready with a quip.

"Our separation was a failure", he explained.

Before long, Yoko was pregnant. John was ecstatic. He fussed over Yoko's pregnancy, taking time out only to assist with his ongoing legal battle to remain in the United States.

Thanks to his lawyers, John had not been deported, despite intense pressure from high government officials to ship him back to Britain.

On 7 October 1975, the U.S. Court of Appeals overturned the order to kick John out of the country. All indications were that Lennon could now stay in the U.S. without fear of being deported.

Two days later, Yoko gave birth to Sean Ono Lennon in New York Hospital. The baby arrived right on John's 35th birthday.

While his first son, Julian, had been unplanned – and largely unloved – by his father, John was determined to make good with his second child. He announced that he was through with his solo career. From now on, John told the press, he would make dinner, not music.

Chapter 10 Starting Over

With the assistance of several staff members, John spent the rest of the 1970s tending to Sean. While John had barely acknowledged his first son, he showered Sean with affection and costly presents. Some said Sean was spoiled. Lennon didn't mind; he enjoyed indulging his son's every whim.

The next few years passed quietly, though they were punctuated by a few dramatic highs and lows.

In March 1976, John's father died of stomach cancer in a British charity hospital ward. John contacted Freddie shortly before he died. He was willing to forget his animosity towards his father and console him on the phone.

In July of that same year, John was finally granted permanent resident's status in the United States.

During the spring of 1977, the Lennons made the first of several visits to Japan. Yoko was eager to reconcile with her estranged family. The visits weren't always smooth, but Yoko was glad of the opportunity to get reacquainted with her kin.

The most dramatic development in this period was John and Yoko's role reversal. Yoko became actively involved in handling John's business affairs. She began attending high-powered meetings and negotiating pricey deals. John stayed at home and looked after Sean. When he wasn't babysitting, he got stoned and watched the television.

After Sean was born, Lennon largely stopped writing music. But in the spring of 1980, while relaxing on a family holiday to Bermuda, John felt the first stirrings of his long suppressed talent. Perhaps the beautiful weather and lovely scenery inspired him. For the first time in years, he began writing new songs.

At some point during his sojourn, John contacted Yoko, who had remained in New York City. Yoko was pleased to hear that John was writing tunes again. Yoko had a surprise announcement of her own. She had also begun to work on some new songs. Yoko suggested that she and John combine forces and put together an album featuring their compositions. Lennon agreed.

Once he returned to New York, John entered a recording studio called the Hit Factory, eager to reconquer the music world. For a change, the producer was Jack Douglas, not Phil Spector.

The album John and Yoko laboured on was designed for two purposes. It would relaunch John's career and make a pop star out of Yoko. Aware of the violent disdain in which critics and fans held her, Yoko demanded that her husband fashion her a hit single. John had enjoyed a slew of hits, so it was only fair, in her eyes.

John and Yoko didn't spend all their time in the recording studio. They also had to hustle to get a new record contract. John had let his old contract lapse when he withdrew from the music business. Record company officials were eager to sign John up, but were less than thrilled when they discovered he planned on giving several tracks to his wife.

Fans and critics unanimously hated Yoko's shrieky music. Her songs were regarded as a bad joke. All of her solo albums had flopped, despite John's strong support.

The Lennons eventually signed with David Geffen of Geffen Records. He was virtually the only record company executive willing to take a chance on a John and Yoko collaboration album.

John and Yoko's comeback album bore the title *Double Fantasy*. The first single from the album, 'Starting Over', was released in October.

"Starting Over" was not one of John's best numbers. It was a pleasant pop ditty that actually sounded like something Paul McCartney could have written. Nonetheless, fans were ecstatic, for the song represented the first new tune released by John since the mid-1970s.

Yoko arranged for a massive public relations blitz to accompany the release of John's new single and upcoming album. Lennon gave in-depth interviews to the likes of *Playboy* magazine, in which he talked about life as a househusband and his decision to return to the musical mainstream.

John was bubbling over with ideas. He even fancied conducting a concert tour, playing old and new material. After half a decade, John was returning in triumph to the world of rock 'n' roll.

* * *

John's comeback coincided with the release of a scathing profile in *Esquire* magazine. The article made it clear that John was a very wealthy man. The magazine story portrayed John as an out-of-touch hippie with a huge bank account.

To many people, this reeked of hypocrisy. John's persona was that of a peace-loving hippie with no regard for the material world. After all, this was the man whose song "Imagine" idealized the notion of having no possessions.

One reader in particular was infuriated by the piece. His name was Mark David Chapman – and he hated hypocrites.

A plump, bespectacled, 25-year-old security guard in Hawaii, Chapman had been a huge Beatles fan while growing up in the U.S. state of Georgia. At 17, however, Chapman underwent a dramatic religious conversion. He renounced rock music and stopped taking drugs. He cut his long hair, began attending church and worked as a summer camp counsellor for the YMCA.

Around the same time he was converting to religion, Chapman became obsessed with the novel *The Catcher in the Rye* by J.D. Salinger. The book details the misadventures of Holden Caulfield, a prep school dropout, who decides to visit the seedy underbelly of New York City. Caulfield hates pretense and "phoney" people. So did Chapman, who strongly identified with Caulfield's quest for truth.

Three years after discovering *The Catcher in the Rye*, Chapman entered a religious college, intent on securing credentials that would enable him to rise in the YMCA hierarchy. He found the pressures of studying too much, however, and had a nervous breakdown. Chapman dropped out after one semester.

During the late 1970s, Chapman visited Hawaii. He attempted to commit suicide there, and was briefly committed to a mental hospital. After being released in 1978, Chapman embarked on a round-the-world tour. While on this global trek, he met and married a Japanese girl named Gloria Abe.

In late 1979, Chapman took a position as a security guard. He was living in Hawaii again and seemed to be settling down.

Had his bosses been more attentive, they might have hesitated to hire Chapman as a guard. Chapman believed that God and Satan spoke to him on a regular basis. These supreme beings held lengthy conversations inside Chapman's head, in which they urged him to do something about "phonies" like John Lennon. When the voices in his head became too persistent to ignore, Chapman quit his job and purchased a five shot .38 calibre revolver in Honolulu.

In late October 1980, Chapman flew to New York City. There, he visited all the sites that Holden Caulfield toured in *The Catcher in the Rye.*

While he brought his revolver on his trip, Chapman wasn't able to use it. Much to his annoyance, Chapman discovered he needed a permit to buy bullets in New York. To get around this problem, he took a trip to Atlanta, Georgia, where an old friend supplied him with five hollow-nosed bullets.

Chapman returned to Hawaii, where he showed off his pistol to his increasingly concerned wife. He talked openly about killing John Lennon and about the voices in his head. Gloria urged him to get counselling. Reluctantly, Chapman made an appointment with a therapist. He never kept it.

On 5 December 1980 Chapman left Hawaii and returned to New York. He rented a room at a local YMCA and began touring the city, checking out the Dakota apartments, among other locales.

Meanwhile, Lennon was experiencing something of renaissance. Though *Double Fantasy* (which had been released that autumn) was struggling in the charts, John was delighted to hear his new songs played on the radio. Feeling stable and rejuvenated, he made an effort to reach out to old friends and acquaintancces. He decided to help Ringo with an album, and even wrote a song for the former Beatles drummer. The tune was called “Nobody Told Me There'd Be Days Like These”.

Lennon also had an ambitious plan to re-record his best-known Beatles songs. John felt that George Martin never quite achieved the exact sound he was looking for and he wanted the opportunity to redo some of his tunes.

In early December, John conducted an interview with a reporter from the BBC. He shrugged when asked a question about his personal security. “I can go right out this door now and go into a restaurant”, John told the reporter. “You want to know how great that is?”

Lennon made it clear he wasn't interested in having a bodyguard.

* * *

On the morning of 8 December 1980, John took part in an elaborate photo session with the famous photographer Annie Leibovitz. The session, which took place in the Dakota itself, would provide the images for a cover story in an upcoming edition of *Rolling Stone*.

Among other poses, John was pictured naked, lying next to a fully clothed Yoko. In the photograph, he was curled up in the foetal position, making him look like a huge, nude infant. Lennon was delighted with the shot, stating that it neatly summed up his relationship with Yoko.

Once the photo session was over, John conducted an interview with a disc jockey. He recounted the now familiar tale of his decision to drop out of the music business and look after Sean.

After the interview, John and Yoko left the Dakota to head to the studio. It was roughly 5 p.m. The winter sky was already dark and, as usual, a small knot of fans was waiting in front of the Dakota when the Lennons stepped outside. A pudgy young man with glasses held out a copy of *Double Fantasy* for John to sign, which he did. A photographer snapped a picture of the event. The photo captured John in the foreground and Mark David Chapman in the background, peering anxiously at the ex-Beatle.

Chapman seemed delighted to have had his album autographed. He chatted excitedly with the Dakota doorman and other complete strangers about his encounter with Lennon. He looked to all the world like just an ordinary, enthusiastic fan.

But inside Chapman's head the voices of God and Satan were debating the merits of shooting John Lennon. In his coat pocket was his loaded .38 calibre revolver. While the powers of good and evil deliberated in his head, Chapman watched John and Yoko climb into a limo and drive off.

Chapman stayed by the Dakota, a beatific grin on his chubby face, waiting for the former Beatle to return.

At the studio, the Lennons listened to playbacks of a

Yoko composition called "Walking On Thin Ice". The tune featured a boppy disco beat, heavy guitar and Yoko's inimitable vocals. Mindful of his wife's desire to be a hit maker, Lennon had lavished an unusual amount of care on this song. With some heavy promotion, John and Yoko were convinced the tune would be a chart topper.

As John tinkered with the recording of "Walking On Thin Ice", Chapman continued his vigil at the Dakota. By 10:50 p.m., the argument inside his head had exploded into full-blown mania. Unable to sort out which voice was God and which Satan, Chapman turned his attention to the limousine pulling up to the curb.

He watched John Lennon's wife, Yoko, step onto the pavement. The legend himself followed shortly after, holding some cassette tapes in his hands.

Chapman greeted the famous pair with a "hello". He saw Lennon look at him with searching eyes, felt the man peer into his mind and read his thoughts. The Lennons brushed past Chapman and headed towards the entrance of the Dakota. With his back to Chapman, John never saw the former Christian youth leader reach into his coat pocket and withdraw his .38.

Chapman assumed a combat stance, then fired all five rounds at point-blank range.

The first two shots hit John in the back. Two more rounds smacked into his shoulder. One shot missed its target completely. John dropped the tapes in his hand and staggered into the front security office of the Dakota, trailing blood.

"John's been shot!" Yoko screamed, as Jay Hastings, the night watchman, looked on in horror. Hastings hit an alarm button on his desk to alert the police, then rushed to aid John, whose torso was covered in blood.

Police arrived at the Dakota within minutes. They found an hysterical Yoko begging for a doctor to save her husband. The police also found Mark David Chapman, standing calmly by the Dakota, reading a copy of *The Catcher in the Rye.* Police drew their guns on the assassin and hauled him off to a nearby station.

Other police officers gingerly lifted Lennon into the back of a squad car. The car then rushed to Roosevelt hospital where a team in the emergency room tried frantically to stem John's bleeding. Despite the heroic efforts of seven medical officials, doctors were unable to revive John, who had lost over three-quarters of his blood.

On 8 December 1980, at 11:07 p.m., John Winston Lennon was pronounced dead. He was just 40 years old.

* * *

Tributes to John poured in following his death.

"John Lennon helped create the mood and the music of the time", said then President Jimmy Carter in a press statement. "I am saddened by his death and distressed by the senseless manner of it".

"It was a staggering moment when I heard the news", said Frank Sinatra. "Lennon was a most talented man and, above all, a gentle soul".

Writer Norman Mailer described Lennon as "a genius of the spirit" while rocker Chuck Berry said John "had a white face but a black man's soul".

George Harrison and Ringo Starr were both initially too upset to speak to the press. They made brief statements through their spokespersons expressing shock and horror.

Paul McCartney managed to get a few words in to reporters, but he too showed signs of shock at the death of his old mate.

"I can't take it at the moment", Paul told journalists. "John was a great guy. He's going to be missed by the whole world".

Fans, too, paid their respects to the slain Beatle. On 14 December 1980, a vigil was held around the world to mark John's death. One hundred thousand people packed into Central Park in New York City where they observed 10 minutes of silence.

Yoko Ono made one of the more poignant statements in the days following the shooting. "Sean cried", Yoko stated. "He also said, 'Now Daddy is part of God. I guess when you die you become bigger, a part of everything'". She added, "John loved and prayed for the human race. Please do the same for him".

Epilogue

John Lennon was a brilliant songwriter, a bad husband and a failed father, as far as Julian and Cynthia were concerned. He sang of peace while experiencing little of it in his private life. He sang of love while bearing intensely bitter feelings about his childhood.

Sean and Yoko knew a different man, no less complicated, but overwhelmingly present with his love and with his need. If Julian and Cynthia suffered from absence and neglect, Sean and Yoko experienced enough Lennon to last a lifetime. They needed it.

And then there was the Lennon the press knew: the "smart Beatle", the poet and the visionary who knew the depth of his own genius, who conquered the music charts and failed at the music business, who fell for some very silly schemes.

John Lennon had a talent for chaos. He was born into it, he spread it and he had no idea how to master it, except in one regard: he articulated chaos – through his words and his songs – better than anyone else of his generation. "Life", said Lennon, "is what happens to you when you're busy making other plans".

While Lennon made other plans, millions of fans were moved by his music. EMI estimates that the Beatles have sold over one billion albums, tapes, singles and CDs – making them the most successful group of all time.

In their short career, the Beatles continuously set the pace for pop music. They rejuvenated a dormant music scene in the United Kingdom and were the first British band to dominate the U.S. charts. The Beatles' success paved the way for countless other British groups who made it big in America.

Rubber Soul heralded the arrival of folk-rock while *Revolver* and *Sergeant Pepper* popularised psychedelic music. Every subsequent album proved the Beatles' willingness to innovate and explore.

At the peak of their stardom, when their celebrity threatened to overwhelm their music, the Beatles stopped touring and withdrew, fulltime, to the studio. In the process, they proved that rock albums could be art.

Despite their reclusion, the Beatles' influence only grew. Millions of teenagers grew their hair after seeing the mop tops in action. The Beatles popularised Eastern mysticism and, for better or worse, inspired countless youths to turn on, tune in and drop out.

After the Beatles, the impact of Lennon's musical output waxed and waned while the power of his persona grew apace. With Yoko Ono at his side, Lennon became a revolutionary and a clown whose weird and wonderful peace projects made up in brilliance what they lacked in reason.

Even as Lennon's professional and personal twists left

fans bewildered, his best compositions became anthems for their times.

John Lennon has continued to leave his mark, even after his death. In 1994, the remaining Beatles got together to add additional vocals and music on a pair of demo tracks that Lennon had never properly recorded. The release of two "new" Beatles songs – "Free As a Bird" and "Real Love" – delighted fans around the world.

Ironically, John himself was dismissive of the Beatles' success. In his shattering *Rolling Stone* interview of 1970, Lennon poured scorn on fans who held the Beatles in idolatrous worship. "I met Paul and said, 'Do you want to join me band?' And then George joined and then Ringo joined. We were just a *band* who made it very, very big – that's all".

Further Reading

Draper, Robert. *Rolling Stone Magazine: The Uncensored History*. New York: Doubleday, 1990.

The Editors of *Rolling Stone* magazine. *The Ballad of John and Yoko*. New York: Rolling Stone Press, 1982.

Goldman, Albert. *The Lives of John Lennon*. New York: William Morrow and Company, 1988.

Kendall, Brian. *Our Hearts Went Boom: The Beatles Invasion of Canada*. Toronto: Penguin Books Canada, 1997.

Marchbank, Pearce. *John Lennon: In His Own Words*. New York: Quick Fox, 1981.

McCabe, Peter and Schonfeld, Robert. *Apple To the Core*. New York: Pocket Books, 1972.

Wenner, Jann, editor. *Lennon Remembers*. London: Verso, 2000.

Wenner, Jann, editor. *20 Years of Rolling Stone Magazine: What a Long Strange Trip It's Been.* New York: Straight Arrow Publishers, 1987.

Williams, Allan and Marshall, William. *The Man Who Gave the Beatles Away.* New York: Ballantine Books, 1975.

About the Author

Nate Hendley is a freelance writer who lives in Toronto, Canada. He is the author of *Edwin Alonzo Boyd: The Life and Crimes of Canada's Master Bank Robber* and *The Black Donnellys: The Outrageous Story of Canada's Deadliest Feud.*

His website is located at www.natehendley.com.

Hendley lives with two demanding cats and a wonderful girlfriend named Alyson.

Acknowledgements

I wish to thank Altitude Publishing for their continued support, my family for their constant encouragement and my girlfriend, Alyson, for her patience and love. I also wish to thank Cheryl Lajoie for her strong interest in my book. I am sorry that she never got the chance to read it.

Most of the quotes that appear in this book were made by John himself and were published in a variety of sources. These include *The Ballad of John and Yoko*, a compilation of *Rolling Stone* magazine articles and interviews with Lennon, *John Lennon In His Own Words*, which, as the title implies, consists of a long series of memorable quotes from Chairman John, and most of all, *Lennon Remembers*, the complete transcript of the infamous interviews Lennon conducted with *Rolling Stone* editor Jann Wenner.

Other quotes by and about Lennon were culled from articles in such newspapers as *The Globe and Mail*, *The Toronto Star* and *The Kitchener-Waterloo Record*. For the most part, the newspaper stories I used in this book were originally published in late 1980, following John's murder.

I am also indebted to Albert Goldman's highly controversial, but extremely detailed, tome, *The Lives of John Lennon*. The latter provided a wealth of information about John's business dealings and solo career (not to mention, several caustic broadsides about Lennon's musical talent).

Amazing Author Question and Answer

What was your inspiration for writing about John Lennon?

I am a lifelong Beatles fan and have always admired John Lennon's wit, charisma and songwriting ability. I've got a mass of Beatles/Lennon records and books, so when the opportunity presented itself to write about John, I seized the moment.

What surprised you most while you were researching John Lennon?

I found it interesting how John always seemed to need a "supporting partner" in his life, be it Paul, Stu Sutcliffe, Yoko or, when he was younger, his mother, Julia.

What do you most admire about John Lennon?

Lennon's creative consistency. From roughly 1962 to 1972, Lennon put out a continuous stream of incredible pop songs. What's truly fascinating is how his music changed over the years and how he was capable of writing tunes in so many different genres.

What escapade do you most identify with?

John's matrimonial troubles.

What difficulties did you run into when researching John Lennon?

I found it difficult to write objectively about Yoko, because she triggers such strong negative reactions in people (including me).

What part of the writing process did you enjoy most?

Being able to revisit all my favourite Lennon/Beatle songs in the name of research.

Why did you become a writer? Who inspired you?

I've wanted to be a writer since I was a young child. My parents, peers and a few assorted teachers (especially my grade eight teacher, Ken Quanz, who took the time to read and critique my earliest "novellas") served as my initial inspiration.

What is your next project?

I am working on a book about Al Capone for Altitude. I very much enjoy the crime genre as it lends itself to colourful prose – sort of like music writing.